Humour, Heart and Hope: Life in Walmgate

Van Wilson
with additional photography by
Simon I Hill FRPS

Published by the
Archaeological Resource Centre
St Saviourgate, York

with the support of

The Scirebröc Group
and
York Oral History Project

1996

Published by the Archaeological Resource Centre
St Saviourgate, York

7 December 1996

British Library Cataloguing in Publication Data
The Catalogue Record for this book is available from the British Library

ISBN No.   1 874454 14 0

Design and layout is by The Scirebröc Group, York. Tel 01904 672350
Printing is by Quacks, York. Tel 01904 635967

Please note: *for reasons of economy this book has been 'perfect bound'. Breaking the spine of the book will damage the binding and may result in pages becoming separated from the book.*

Cover photograph
Alexandra Yard, Walmgate, 1933

Contents

List of Illustrations

(including source, or photographer, if known)

i

Foreword

For most visitors, York is the Minster and the Shambles, the Heritage Centres and the teddy-bear shops. But beyond Foss Bridge is another and very different York, one which few tourists see: Walmgate, one of the only residential areas within the city walls. When I first came to York in 1965, Walmgate was still talked of with a mixture of delighted horror and sly pride. It was, my Heslington neighbours told me, the street where policemen only ventured in twos and threes on a Saturday night. By then 'old Walmgate' had in fact changed completely, and today it is perhaps the quietest part of the city.

Yet there are (thank heavens) many who remember old Walmgate. With their help, Van Wilson has produced this splendidly readable account of a richly diverse community and the characters who provided its unique flavour. This is not, however, a sentimental book about the 'good old days'. Colour and warmth Walmgate certainly had, but also hunger, tragedy and sometimes grinding poverty, only just made bearable by kindness and good neighbourliness and even local pride. Nobody in their right sense would want Walmgate's hunger and poverty back, but Walmgate's sense of community, still just surviving, is a thing to be treasured and nurtured.

Dr Charles Kightley
Churchwarden, St Denys', Walmgate

Introduction

Since the publication of 'Rich in all but Money : Life in Hungate 1900-1938' in February 1996, which was the story of a lost area of York, many people have asked for a similar book on the adjoining area of Walmgate. Following an article in the Yorkshire Evening Press, I have talked to over sixty people about their memories of this part of York.

I would not claim that this is a definitive history of Walmgate, indeed it can probably do no more than scratch the surface. For reasons of space and economy I have had to be highly selective in the editing of both my own work and of the material provided by the people interviewed. But their stories, which together paint a fascinating portrait of a place which has changed enormously over the last half-century, are now stored on tape and written transcript, in the archives of the York Oral History Project, where they will remain for posterity.

In choosing what to include and what to omit, I have to admit to a personal preference for the history of people and their lives, rather than that of streets and buildings. There is mention of many places and businesses, but most of the text is concerned with the lives of the ordinary men and women who have, over the years, made up the population of this exciting and vibrant part of our city.

As in any work of this kind, there are a number of people whose support and help have been invaluable. Special thanks are due to those whose stories appear in the text. They are profiled on the next few pages. I would also like to thank the following who have shared information : Ivy Barker and Gladys Evans, Stan Beddingham, Dolly Corrigan, Mrs Davies, Mr M Doran, Olive Hardy, Jimmy Mullen, Alf Ottaway, Mrs Starkey, Gladys Terry, David Wilde.

For help with interviews in the early stages or for answers to specific queries, I wish to thank : Joe Boutflower, Janet Cowper, Gill Craddock and Muriel Randles of the York Oral History Project; Brian Hardyman,

Dick Hunter, Margaret O'Donnell, Ron Powell and John Sweeney. For access to archives and information about the area, I must thank : Rita Freedman, Philip Johnson and staff of the York City Archives; the staff of York City Reference Library; Sister Gregory at the Bar Convent Museum; Staff of the Council for British Archaeology; Norman Fowler and Sandra Vardy for access to St George's School registers; Victoria Osborne of York City Art Gallery; Diana Lay of the Bass Museum; Andrew Davison, Inspector of Ancient Monuments for English Heritage; and Chris Titley of the Yorkshire Evening Press.

I would like to thank Paul Fox of City of York Council for access to Walmgate Bar; the staff of Ellerkers; Mr Bill Stubbs and Henry Duncan of Stubbs the Ironmongers; Graham Acaster of Acaster Transport; Dave Jarvis, Warehouse Manager of Yorkshire Evening Press; Andrew 'Bone' Jones, Ruth Dass, Ian Fisher, Ian Carlisle, Martin Bartlett and staff of the ARC; Lol Barker, Hugh Murray and Joe Murphy for the loan of photographs.

My particular thanks to Charles Kightley for kindly writing the foreword and for supplying information about St Denys's church; Brenda Allison of St Denys's for her support and enthusiasm; Alan Hardwick and Colin Lea of the York Oral History Project; David Poole for assistance with research and for sharing some of his encyclopaedic knowledge of York people; Wendy Sherlock, Editor with the York Archaeological Trust, for reading the text and making suggestions; and The Scirebröc Group, Patricia & Peter Shepherd Trust, Sheldon Memorial Trust, and York Common Good Trust for financial support.

Most of all, I am particularly indebted to two colleagues: Simon I Hill, for copying the old photographs, for his excellent new photography and his continual support; and Mike Race for help with interviews and research, and for reading the manuscript and making useful suggestions.

THIS BOOK IS DEDICATED TO ALL THOSE MEN AND WOMEN
WHO HAVE LIVED IN THE WALMGATE AREA

Profiles of Walmgate Residents

Thomas Abbot was born in 1919 and lived in King's Yard, Walmgate. He attended St Denys's church.

Malcolm Ainsworth was born in 1936 in Chapel Row, went to St George's school and played rugby for several teams. He remembers the Newcastle Arms and is still a member of the INL club.

Mrs **Maureen Aspinall** was born in 1934 in Hull, moved to Walmgate as a baby and lived there for most of her life. She is the youngest of 13 children, and her family owned a second-hand shop.

Frederick Atkinson was born in Alma Terrace in 1913, moved to Paragon Street in 1922 and has vivid memories of the cattle market.

Noel Attree was born in 1914 at the Red Lion, Merchantgate and lived there until he was 17. He is still a keen member of St George's church.

Kenneth Barton was born in 1918. His mother was employed by the Corporation to work on a food programme for the poor children of Walmgate. He now lives in Fulford.

Mrs **Mary Booker** was born in 1910 in Navigation Road, the daughter of an Irish mother and English father.

Arthur Brown worked at Isaac Poad's for 60 years, from junior to Director. A pupil of Archbishop Holgate's Grammar School, he has been a boxing coach, and director of York City football club.

Mrs **Eileen Brown** was born in 1914, the daughter of Len Holgate, who owned the first motorised cattle vehicle in York. Her mother was descended from the O'Donnells who came from Ireland in 1840s.

Mrs **Joyce Burnett** was born in 1926 in Clock Yard, Walmgate. Her mother looked after a home and family, worked in a shop, had a cleaning job, was a bookie's runner, and read the tea-leaves.

Richard (Dick) Calpin was born in Rosemary Place in 1909. His family came from North Mayo in Ireland during the potato famine. He met his wife in Walmgate and now lives in Heworth.

Owen Calpin was born in the 1920s in Long Close Lane, one of eleven children. Members of his family ran the INL club for many years.

Stanley Cowen was born in 1922, attended St Margaret's school and started part-time work in Walmgate at the age of eleven.

Ray D lived off George Street from 1925 to 1936 and met his wife at the Malt Shovel public house. He later returned and ran a transport business in the area.

Mrs **Mary Dent** was born in 1914, and lived in Walmgate from 1940 to 1964 with her husband at Dent's butchers, the family business for over 50 years.

Brian Douglass attended St George's school from 1936 to 1943, but lived at the Greyhound hotel in Coney Street. He has strong memories of the school and the church.

Mrs **Ethel Pretoria (Tory) Dunnington** was born in 1900 and lived in Dixon's Yard from 1915 to 1931. She still has affiliations with St Denys's church.

Mrs **Rona Eaton** was born in 1917 and attended Fishergate school. She had friends in Walmgate. Although now living in Exeter, she has very fond memories of York.

Brian Fletcher runs the Walmgate post office. For many years he was in charge of St George's youth/social club, and now organises activities at St Lawrence's.

Miss **Rita Graham** worked at Crow's butchers from 1951 to 1957, and remembers Walmgate as a child when her grandma lived there.

Anthony Gray is the nephew of the directors of Crow's butchers. After some years in the CID, he took over the family business in its later years. He now lives in Stamford Bridge.

Albert Howard was born in 1913 and lived in Long Close Lane. Whilst at St Denys's school, he won the school swimming championship and was known for his singing voice.

Mrs **Mary Jeffrey** was born in 1916 and lived in Chapel Row. Her husband Ron Jeffrey worked for Beaumonts bakers during the war. She remembers a lot about shops and St George's girls' school.

Terry Kilmartin was born in 1928 and lived in Huby's Passage and the lodging-house run by his grandfather. He is an active member of St George's church and the St Vincent de Paul society.

Henry King began work at the age of thirteen between the wars, for the hairdresser and tobacconist T Croft & Sons. He spent two days a week on the tobacco stall in the cattle market.

Reg Lambert started St Lawrence's school in 1925. His family worked in Walmgate and he now lives in Acomb.

Stan Lea was born in 1909 and lived in the Manor House, Dixon's Yard, and attended St Denys's church where he excelled at sport.

Stan Leaf, an ex-policeman, was landlord of the Phoenix from 1953 to 1963 when most of his clientele came from the cattle market.

Harry Lovick was born in Walmgate in 1924 and managed the draper's shop which his parents had started up in 1915.

Mrs **Vera Lyall** was landlady of the Lord Nelson Inn from 1957 to 1962, and talks about the interesting people who came into the pub.

Mrs **Ina Paterson** is the great-grand-daughter of Macy Ann Boulton who was caretaker of Navigation School and the local midwife, attending many Irish wives of itinerant labourers.

Mrs **Annie Pinder** was born in Hope Street in 1904, and her parents came from Sligo in the 1850s. She recalls her mother working in the potato fields during the day and doing housework at night.

Mrs **Betty Pollard** and Mrs **Pat Daker** are grand-daughters of Ralph Ellerker, the founder of Ellerkers saddle and rope shop. Betty Pollard was born there in 1925, but her younger sister Pat was born in Heslington Lane, though both remember living and helping in the shop.

Mrs **Elsie Precious** (nee **Strangeway**) was born in 1900, and her family owned the hay and straw business in George Street which supplied the cattle market.

Mrs **Lillian Prior** was born in Farrar Street in 1914 and attended St Lawrence's school. Her uncle had a coal business in Walmgate.

Mrs **Violet Quigley** was born in 1912 and has lived in Hope Street and Long Close Lane. Her husband Jeff was well-known in the area.

Michael Race was born in 1938 and lived in Dundee Street, off Lawrence Street. He attended St George's school and church and spent most of his youth in the Walmgate area.

Mrs **Rubye Readhead** was born in George Street in 1924 and attended Castlegate school. She remembers many of the colourful characters in the area.

Tom Rhodes was born in Willow Street in 1910, after his family migrated from Ireland in 1853. He attended St George's church and school.

Richard Sanderson was born in 1929 in St Peter's Vaults on the corner of Willow Street, where his grandfather was landlord.

Peter Stanhope originates from Bishophill but his relatives, the Gibsons, had a shoe and boot shop in Walmgate and were all baptised at St Margaret's church.

Mrs **Betty Thompson** recalls her grandparents who owned Cambages greengrocers in Walmgate from 1900 to the 1930s.

Andy Waudby was born in 1921 in Hungate, but later moved to live near Walmgate Bar. He played in Walmgate and also earned money singing Irish songs in the streets.

Mrs **Olive Waudby** was born in 1909 in the Shambles but her family moved to Walmgate, where she worked for Fotheringham's plumbers. Her late husband, Wilf Waudby, owned the fishmongers in Walmgate.

Mrs **Sheila White** was born in 1925 at her grandmother's off-licence and later ran several pubs and the off-licence on the corner of Albert Street and Walmgate in the 1960s.

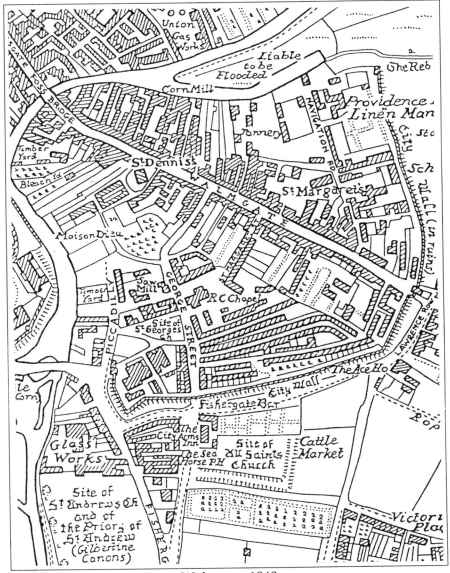

Walmgate 1849

1

Setting the Scene

Perhaps more than any other area of York, Walmgate has a reputation for being colourful, vibrant and full of life, and the microcosm of the city. Churches, pubs, shops, factories, schools, a police cell, and houses ranging from the Georgian residence at Number 70 to the tiny back-to-backs of Long Close Lane, were all encompassed in one single district.

In the 19th and early 20th centuries, the road from Foss Bridge to Walmgate Bar was the scene of 600 yards of bustling life. On the main road and in the many streets, alleyways, yards and courts leading off from it, have lived thousands of men and women, involved in every aspect of work. In 1900, for example, there were innkeepers, timber merchants, firemen, cattle drovers, hairdressers, policemen, engineers, grocers, and everything in between, as well as the less common keelman, lamplighter, tripe dealer, combmaker, prison warder and Chief Rabbi.

As far as entertainment was concerned, York's first purpose-built cinema, the Electric (built in 1911) was just over the bridge in Fossgate, and there were also social clubs, a working-men's club, and sports teams, not to mention the preponderance of pubs and beer shops to be found in this part of York.

Much has been written about the strong Irish community who lived in this area from the mid-19th century into the 1930s. But in Walmgate there were also Russians, Italians, Chinese and other races living amongst those who originated from nearer home. There were Catholics, Protestants, Jews, and one or two other religions. On the whole these different groups tended to mix together reasonably well, though there were certainly incidences of prejudice and racism, particularly before the

Second World War. Today many of these groups have assimilated and inter-married with their host group, and most of the population have moved on, being rehoused during the 1930s and 1950s clearances.

Walmgate

Medieval Walmgate

Right from medieval times, Walmgate, or Walbagate as it was called, was an important street. It had six churches: St Denys, St Margaret, St Mary, St George, St Edward the Martyr and St Peter le Willow, of which only the first two remain. In 1547, various York parishes were amalgamated, St George was united with St Denys, and later St George's RC church was built in George Street. In the 17th and early 18th centuries, it was quite a prosperous area and there were many attractive houses used as town residences by wealthy families. Once it became safe to move outside the walls, and protection was no longer needed, these residents left the area and rented out their properties until speculators came along and bought them, in order to build many more houses on the sites.

Percy's Inn, the home of the Earls of Northumberland, was demolished and a group of cottages built in its place. Mr Stan Lea lived in one down Dixon's Yard, called the Manor House,

A big six-roomed house, we was the only one in that yard that had a toilet indoors. And that was a lot in them days. Three big bedrooms and a sitting room, a kitchen and a living-room. There was yard to put washing in if it was fair weather.

His sister, Mrs Tory Dunnington also recalls the house,

Our landlord was Leethams and they asked if we'd like to go to Manor House and we went there in 1915 and stayed until 1931. At the bottom was the river and facing there was Leethams Mill.

The stairs were wider than a yard, the staircase took thirteen rolls of paper and all down the sides there was black heavy fittings. Lovely rail to get hold of. In the hall it was all tiles and shelves where you could put plants. There was railings along and me mam used to have a few flowers planted and a bed of mint. It was a lovely house.

Almshouses

Among the almshouses in the area, two are of particular interest. Winterscales Hospital, named after Percival Winterscale, Sheriff of York in 1705, was a timber-framed building in Walmgate, possibly of the 15th century, down a lane next to Bowes Morrell House. It was designed to provide for six of the 'poor of St Margaret's parish', chosen by the churchwardens, to receive £8 a year. The building was demolished in 1957. In 1710, Dorothy Wilson provided a house on Foss Bridge for ten poor women. She died in 1717 but left money in her will for the almshouse to continue. It was rebuilt in 1765 and again in 1812, and included a schoolroom for 20 poor boys, with a schoolmaster's house at the back. The school closed in 1895 but the hospital continued, at least until further modernisation in 1958. Miss Wilson has a monument above the door in St Denys's church.

Bowes Morrell House

The oldest building in Walmgate is the timber-framed Bowes Morrell House, reputedly the only complete 15th century house in York. It was built about 1400 but had extensions added later. The house is ninety yards west of the site of St Peter le Willow church, and is the only survivor of a group of four. It is thought to have been the vicarage. In the 1930s it became Kilmartin's lodging-house (see chapter 5) and in 1955 there was some mention of demolishing the house but the Ministry of Housing intervened to oppose this. In 1961 the lodging-house was acquired by the Civic Trust. It was officially re-opened on 28th October 1966 as Bowes Morrell House, in memory of JB Morrell, one of the founders of the Trust who had financed the restoration, though he had died in 1963. It is presently occupied by the Council for British Archaeology. Mrs Mary Dent played a part in ensuring that the house was acquired for posterity. She became familiar with the place during the 1940s when she was a Macmillan cancer visitor,

There were all people who'd had gastrectomies, a lot of them through drinking. I used to go into the old lodging-house, and there was this great big gas stove and they were all round it.

Mrs Dent heard that the building might be demolished, so voiced her concerns to Morrell, who contacted the Dean, Milner-White, then asked her to,

Get the chap's name and address who it belonged to. I went on my bicycle and I spoke to Mr Kilmartin and said, 'The Rowntrees Trust are interested in your property'. JB Morrell rang me, 'Will you tell Kilmartin we'll give him £600 for the old lodging-house' and I was cycling to work and he was outside the corporation doors and I told him.

Very few pre-19th century houses remain in Walmgate. Number 70, Norman Collinson House, which now houses Age Concern, is one of the oldest. It has an early 18th century staircase and panelling on the first floor, and a mid 18th century fireplace, although its rainwater head is dated 1783.

In recent years, other parts of the area have been restored by conservationists, like Malt Shovel Court in March 1995. It had been used as fish ponds in medieval times, a red light district in the 19th century, and now its Victorian residences are transformed into luxury apartments.

Walmgate Bar

Walmgate Bar was mentioned as early as the 12th century, although the present Bar dates from the rebuilding of the 14th century. Outside was a moat filled with water and fish. It is the only bar in York with its original barbican, dated 1648, when it was restored following heavy action in the Civil War. There are bullet holes in the limestone face, caused by cannonballs, and in 1836 two unexploded shells were found there. Until 1959 the house over the Bar was private accommodation, for many years a police house. From 1963, it housed the Barbican Bookshop, owned by Dick Rollinson, until it was found that the weight of books was having an adverse affect on the superstructure. By the end of the decade, the space was used for storage purposes only, the shop having moved to its present premises in Fossgate.

Walmgate Bar c1930

View from Walmgate Bar 1996

The thick outer door to the house is covered in metal studs, and through a second door is a room with stone floor, fireplace with stone surround, small latticed windows and portcullis at one end. It was once divided into two, a living area and bedroom. Small doors at two of the corners lead out onto the barbican, where a plaque, signed by the Mayor, Sir William Stephenson, states that the Bar and barbican were restored by the Corporation in 1840.

A wooden staircase leads up to the second floor, which was the second bedroom. The upper part of the portcullis is visible, with its original winding handle. There was no bathroom in the house, leading one to wonder how the family managed. Another set of steps opens out onto the lead roof, with white rail surrounding, once the scene of the family garden. The east turret, now used to store moth-eaten chairs and tools, was once a makeshift cell, which housed local drunkards overnight before they were taken to the police station in the morning.

Rona Eaton remembers visiting the last family to live on the bar,

Inspector Clark and his wife and daughter Dolly lived there. On one occasion I was shown Dolly's bedroom and being quite young at the time, was rather scared when she showed me the portcullis. It was huge and covered almost one wall.

Mary Dent also knew the Clarks,

The turret that they kept the prisoner in was on the left, and she kept the deck-chairs in there so she and her mother could sit on the top in the sun. At one time they'd kept a little piglet in there and then killed it and carried it down as bacon. She said in wartime when there was the bombing, they weren't nervous with the five foot thick walls.

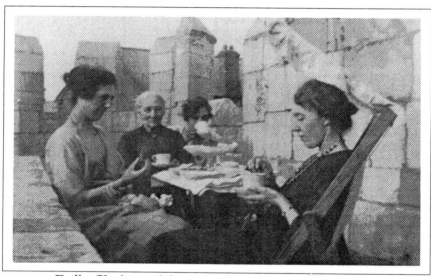

Dolly Clarke and family take tea on Walmgate Bar

In November 1906, the local newspapers were full of the story of Elizabeth Cattle, who had died and was, "the last of four generations to be born in Walmgate Bar, 103 years earlier". Hundreds of mourners lined the route to her funeral at St Margaret's church, which was so well-attended that admission had to be by ticket only. Mrs Cattle was buried in York Cemetery, and her memorial was paid for by Alderman

William Bentley, the Lord Mayor. The lengthy obituary referred to her as York's oldest centenarian, and went on to chart her illustrious career.

In 1885 she was living in Hirst's Yard and advertising her own cure for rheumatism for 1/1 a bottle. As a young woman, she saved the lives of several children, rescuing two from the Foss and one from the Ouse, as well as a boy who had fallen into some manure and was fast sinking beneath it. Notwithstanding the unpleasantness of the consequences, she dived in and pulled him to safety.

But research conducted by local historians David Poole and Hugh Murray has convinced them that Mrs Cattle was not who she thought she was! Before the days of registration, it was difficult for people to be totally accurate about their dates of birth. In more recent times, we have the benefit of census returns and parish registers to aid our research, but in the early part of this century such methods were not available. David Poole's careful study of all the available documents, has located only one possible birthdate for Mrs Cattle, that of November 1814, ten years later than her claim. This would make her only 93 at her death! There is no evidence that an Elizabeth Cattle was born in York between 1803 and 1814, nor that she was born on the Bar. It was probably her uncle who had been custodian.

In 1991, the bar underwent renovations costing £33,000, and various ideas for its use were mooted over the next few years, including a visitor's centre, or a museum, like its counterparts, Monk Bar and Micklegate Bar. The council own the property and are now looking for a suitable tenant.

Clearances

The major clearances in Walmgate took place in 1933-34 when there was a mass exodus to brand new council estates in Tang Hall, Clifton and other parts of the city. Then in October 1955, the York Medical Officer of Health again pronounced many houses in the Walmgate area 'unfit for human habitation' so another batch of CPO's (Compulsory Purchase

Orders) appeared on many buildings, including the houses from George Street to Margaret Street and a group of houses adjoining Paver Lane.

The second batch of clearances was originally scheduled for 1938 but war intervened and put a stop to the work.

Mike Race recalls,

After the war, the Walmgate area was very very run down. I remember prefabs in Long Close Lane and I used to cut across some waste ground where there was a hollow. I didn't realise at the time but a bomb had fallen during the war. Past the end of Hope Street, there was a row of council houses and property which had been standing derelict since before the war. It was a place which was 'between times'. It had been this vibrant lively place 'till the 30s and then people started to move out to other areas.

In the 1950s and 1960s, some of the original residents returned to the area, when new blocks of flats were built in Hope Street and Navigation Road and the whole area given a much-needed facelift. A more recent development is Bretgate, a block of flats and maisonettes masterminded by York Housing Association, designed by John McNeil and built by Claxton and Garland, to house ninety people. The block stretches from Saddler's old lodging-house, round the corner into Navigation Road. On 17th October 1981 it was opened by Viscount Esher, to the accompaniment of the Railway Institute band. The award-winning sheltered apartments took their name from the ancient title of Navigation Road, called Little Bretgate in the 14th century.

Foss Bridge

At the other end of the street is Foss Bridge, built by Peter Atkinson Junior in 1811. The first bridge on the site was wooden, and was replaced by a stone one in 1403. This was the site of the 'fish shambles' in medieval times. Small iron rings can still be seen on the bridge, used for tethering pigs for the Saturday pig market, and at other times used for the goose fair.

2

Three Parishes

At one time Walmgate was the scene of six churches. Today there are three, only two of which still hold services. They all had schools nearby, and one had a thriving social club. St George's primary moved to Fishergate in 1977 and the others have closed.

St Margaret's

St Margaret's Church, first mentioned in the 1150s, has a Norman doorway (with the signs of the Zodiac) which came from St Nicholas's leper hospital in Lawrence Street. During the civil war, the church suffered some attacks, and in the late 17th century, the tower and roof were destroyed in a storm, being rebuilt in 1852. One of the many plaques in the church commemorates Samuel Wormald and his family. Wormald's Cut, the Foss landing-stage behind the Yorkshire Evening Press, was named after the proprietor of the Foss Navigation Company, who was also a timber merchant, shipowner and tanner. He died in 1814, aged of 59. In 1955 the parish was incorporated into St Denys's. When new apartments were built in front of the church in 1992, the Navigation Road Resident's Assoc. protested that twelve leylandii trees had been chopped down in the process. During the 1970s York Civic Trust designated Walmgate a conservation area and funded the restoration of both this church (now used as a theatre store) and St Denys's.

Betty Thompson's family attended St Margaret's,

Mother bought a hat one day to go to church, with red cherries on. It started to rain and all the dye ran down her face. She dare not go in to church after the bells stopped ringing, so she went home and my grandmother thought that someone had attacked her as it looked like blood.

Miss Mann, teacher at St Margaret's School 1920s

Margaret Mann Phillips was the daughter of Rev Francis Mann, and lived in St Margaret's rectory on Fulford Road. The previous rectory had been in Walmgate itself, on the site of the Golden Barrel Inn. She helped her mother to run the girls' club and Sunday school classes. She recalls how on Good Friday in 1918, the choir, robed in surplices, would follow the Rector to 'beat the bounds of the Parish'. They carried a large wooden cross and processed from the church into the streets off Walmgate, halting seven times for the seven stations of the cross. They would sing and the Rector would say the Lord's prayer. Sometimes they encountered passers-by who would join the procession, other times there

St Margaret's School Rugby Team with Miss Mann

would be jeering, and mostly they would be faced with respect, as men removed their caps and women crossed themselves.

Dick Calpin was a pupil at St Margaret's school in Navigation Road,

There'd mebbe only be about 40 or 50 in the school altogether from Standard one to Standard 7. I left at 14, I was the head prefect, captain of the cricket and football, and would you believe it, the head gardener, and I don't know anything about it. The schoolmaster used to take us up to Garrow Hill. That was where our allotment was, and we used to go twice a week.

Stan Cowen also attended St Margaret's,

The playground was behind the school and next to the Bar Walls. It must have been a winter's afternoon, it was snowing and I always remember our teacher, her name could have been Miss Waite, singing a song, 'Softly the snowflakes are falling'.

St Denys'

St Denys' church is dedicated to the patron saint of France, who was also the Bishop of Paris. From 1340 it was the church of the Percy family, whose town house was opposite. The vault beneath the church is said to contain the remains of the 3rd Earl who died after the Battle of Towton on Palm Sunday 1461, leading the losing Lancastrian army. The 14th century stained glass is the second best collection in York, after All Saint's, North Street.

The present church is only a part of the original, which was about four times as large. It was damaged in 1644 by a cannon-ball which hit the spire and affected the main part of the church. In the 18th century it had to contend with being struck by lightning, storm damage and the wall collapsing when drains were dug nearby. The tower is more recent, built in Victorian times. The parish was always a peripheral one, never wealthy, despite the patronage of the Percys. However, its taxes in the 15th century were over double those of St Margaret's. The crypt beneath the church was the home for many years of local vagrants. They were given permission to stay there, provided they lit no fires. Unfortunately they did not heed this, and a fire, which could have had the whole building up in flames, was discovered, and the men evicted.

A great number of men in the parish were killed in the First World War and a memorial to them was lovingly painted onto the wall (the poverty of the parish precluded any monument being purchased). The local British Legion branch and church member Jack King built a new memorial in 1995 to mark the 50th anniversary of VE Day.

Today, St Denys' is part of the city centre team of churches, which also includes St Helen's and All Saints' Pavement. It has a special function, as many services are signed for the deaf.

The garden of the demolished church of St George is situated at the bottom of George Street, and was used as extra burial space for St Denys'. At one time it was locked with a large gate at the entrance, but has now been opened up, mainly to allow tourists to view the grave of Dick Turpin.

Albert Howard attended St Denys' church and the school which was situated opposite,

There was seven classes and they allus used to get together in this big long classroom. We used to sing on a morning, allus 'Jerusalem' and I'm not bragging but Mr Birkett, our headmaster, used to say, 'There's only Howard that can sing here. That's right Albert, you get right to t'top, these people don't.

We allus used to go to the church. As I got older, maybe ten, I used to sing in there. Second time I went, clergyman says, 'I could put you in with the choir. You've a good voice.' I used to go twice a week. We had about ten in the choir, dressed up in these robes, the church used to get full.

Mrs Olive Waudby also belonged to St Denys',

I was in the choir from about fourteen right up until I got married. We used to have a Girls' Friendly Society at the church and a tennis club. It was just a collection of teenage girls. We used to meet every Tuesday and make things, knit things, have bazaars and it was quite nice.

Maureen Aspinall's father had his funeral at St Denys',

Me father died 1949 and he always wanted cremating. Me mother was a catholic, and she says, 'No, he can't be cremated, he has to be buried'. I don't know if this was an omen but we had him in the front shop. Me mam did it all out as an altar and we had all these candles, and t'priest come and t'nuns. They used to sit up all night with him for three nights, and somebody opened the shop door and the candle blew over and it set the shop on fire. Then they had to bring the fire engine, blooming hearse outside, fire engine coming down Walmgate, traffic both ways. They had to put lid on me dad and carry him out and lay him on t'street while they put the fire out. They always say it was me dad's wish to be cremated and he was nearly bloody cremated in that shop, I thought he was gonna go up in flames if they hadn't got him out.

Her husband also had his funeral at the church,

All the men from the Leeds wholesale market where he used to go for his fruit, sent all these flowers and filled the church. I put a seat in the churchyard in memory of Geoff and all t'winos used to come on there. Geoff knew them all and they used to say, 'We're just having a drink with Geoff'. Then someone stole it. I come out for work at half past seven and I always used to look at the seat, knowing Geoff was there, and there was a big thick chain, they must have had an axe to get it. I don't know where it went. But he loved it, St Denys' church.

St George's RC Church

St George's catholic church was built in 1848, designed by JA Hansom (of Hansom cab fame), and a girls' school was attached in 1852. The first teachers were the nuns from the Bar Convent and the pupils were predominantly Irish. The early nuns described the scene on their arrival,

A disorderly crowd of little creatures, for the most part bare-footed and bare-headed, shouting and screaming, mounting every available projection upon which they could perch themselves.

Soon the Sisters began to sing, which had the result of calming and quietening the new pupils. In 1872 the school became mixed, and shortly afterwards the convent nuns withdrew and were replaced by lay teachers. In 1888 the Sisters of Charity of St Vincent de Paul came to York and began to teach in the primary school.

In 1897 the school acquired the disused St George's Methodist chapel in Chapel Row (which had been built in 1826). The tablet in the outside wall stated that the buildings were 'remodelled and opened as girls and infant schools on 19th June 1900'.

Noel Attree remembers the school,

I went when I was three on Christmas Day in 1917. There was a great big sandpit, and an old-fashioned carriage with four little white horses, and when it

15

St George's Church Procession 1930s

moved the horses went up and down. And there was some lovely pictures there of the saints. St Peter and Paul, in a huge semi-circle, supposed to be heaven. Very pretty.

Miss Pearson was Head Teacher, and, believe me, she could clout with that cane, she'd knock skin and bone off yer. But although she was so feared, she had such a lot of kindness as well. When she died, the church was full of all her old lads.

Mrs Mary Jeffrey was a pupil at the girl's school,

There was Sister Catherine, she came to be our head teacher. After she'd finished schooling, she used to go round visiting the sick people. The church used to have a procession, the first Sunday in May and we used to come outside and then down Margaret Street, Walmgate, George Street. And all the girls used to be in white dresses, white shoes, white socks, veils. It was lovely. They carried a statue of the Virgin Mary and some carried banners, it was the lovely month of Mary, the Blessed Virgin.

The choir used to go to our school down Chapel Row and practise on a Thursday night and they called the organist Pennett Thompson. He'd wear black pin-striped trousers, black coat and spats. He always used to have a stick, a little dandy kind of a man. I can remember being stood in that playground and Sister Angela, now she was a tartar. When the whistle went in a morning, you used to stand in your lines and she used to come round and look at your boots, you had to polish them, and at the back of your stockings. She used to have cane in her hand, she used to hit your ankles.

Mary Jackson (now Jeffrey) 1934

Maureen Aspinall's experience of the school was not a happy one,

I didn't like school, I didn't like the teachers, they were too strict. When I got married and we went to see the priest and I told him Geoff was not a catholic, he went mad. They let us get married in a catholic church, but I'd no music and I'd no flowers, I wa'nt allowed 'em. I just walked into church, ten minutes I think I was in, married and straight out.

We used to go to church on a Sunday morning. If you didn't go, you got into trouble. I remember this time I hadn't got up for church. Me best friend, Mary Murray, lived in George Street, We were sat in class and teacher used to come round and just pick on you. 'Maureen Payne, did you go to church yesterday?' 'Yes, sister'. 'Who said mass?' 'Father Breen'. 'What time did you go?' 'Eleven o'clock'. 'Mm, that's funny, Father Breen said 9.30 mass'.

I had to come out in class and I got cane of course, I was always getting t'cane. I remember me sisters were at home and I found this nail polish. I'd only be about six or seven and I painted all me nails and then when I showed them it, they said, 'We've no nail polish remover, you'll have to go to school with it on'. And teacher saw it and they put me in the middle of the hall where everybody used to come in a morning to say prayers. 'Look at this child, she's on the wrong road. Look at her nails', and I'd to hold me hands up while everybody looked at me nails. And I was crying because I was only a little lass.

Brian Douglass also went to St George's,

The school was that poor that it wasn't until nearly ten or eleven that we started using pens and paper. And even then it was only on the back of old medical cards. They were very poor but there was never any stealing or bullying. Police never ever came to the school, Sister Catherine sorted everything out. She had a rosary hanging from her right side and a cane hanging from her left side and she didn't hesitate to use that cane. But we didn't behave out of fear but out of respect. We had the good name of the school to consider. Lads used to come to school with their father's trousers just cut off at knees, not even turned up. I remember one lad, I went to call for him and his mother said, 'Look it's his birthday tomorrow.' She opened this tin and there was four butterfly buns. I thought, 'Well what's special about that?' But to them it was a big thing. The night of the Baedeker raid

St George's Church Mayday Procession

on York, Father Breen and Canon O'Connell knelt in the street praying for the people of York.

The St George's primary school registers include details of baptisms and sacraments. The lists for the 1940s to 1950s show a variety of birthplaces for the children at the school, ranging from different parts of England, to Belfast and Derry in Northern Ireland, Ballykinla and Tyrella in County Down, Ballenagh in County Cavan, as well as India and Egypt. The latter children were those of soldiers.

Tom Rhodes recalls,

Our head teacher was Sister Louise. Ooh she was keen, she used to wear a cane out once a week. We were only totties. Sister Magdalen was a lovely little woman, she died when she was 96.

In Dennis Street was a wooden hut and you had to go if you had toothache. I'd be about 8 or 9 and I must have had something wrong with me teeth so I went. You were all youngsters and you were frightened to bloody death. We'd say to t'lad

19

next to you, 'Go on, it's your...'. 'No, it isn't, you were before me' and it carried on like that until they dragged you in. You could hear 'em screaming out. I was sat there and I thought, 'Oh, bugger this, I'm off' and I run out and they all followed. They come round to the houses and seen our parents and they had to take us next morning and she locked the door. So we were sat there, and we were itching, 'How the hell can we get out now?' And they just about dragged you in, 'cos you really was frightened. They used to come out crying and I thought, 'I'm not going in there'. So we opened the window, got through and run away again and eventually they fastened the windows up and you couldn't get out.

St Patrick's Day Concert 1950 (St George's class with Mr Brophy)
Mike Race, middle row, second from left

Sheila White also visited the place,

Across the road was the school clinic. That was a House of Horrors, you never seen or heard anything like it. Today they put notices up and say 'We've been troubled with head lice.' Then you went to the clinic and they shaved every hair off your head. The kids used to cry and scream and then there was the dentist's chair. A dirty old red apron in rubber and they used to just wipe it down from the person before you.

St Patrick's Day concert at St George's School

Mike Race went to St George's school and church,

The teachers were mainly the Sisters of Charity. Miss Coyle was an archetypal schoolmistress with her hair parted down the middle, grey, severe, in a bun, glasses, she had sort of broken teeth. And there was another lady, she used to have a nice way of keeping the class quiet. She'd say, 'Hush, let's listen to the angel's wings.' Mother and I used to go along to eight o'clock mass every day of the week, Benediction on Thursday and Sunday nights, and confessions on a Saturday evening.

Canon O'Connell was the main priest at St George's and there used to be a queue for confessionals. When you went to him, no matter what you confessed, I think if you'd've raided a bank, or been a serial killer, you always got three Hail Mary's.

The church wasn't only a place you used to go to worship, it was also where we lived our social life. Being a member of the church meant going on trips, altar boys used to have camps away and it meant playing football. The priests were very much part of our lives, in some respects almost like surrogate uncles.

Father Breen used to come to our house and he'd talk to me father about horses and me father would go and put a bet on for him. I can't ever remember the priest coming to our house and talking about religion. The only time I ever remember talking to a priest about religion, it was learning Latin responses. If you didn't know them, you'd get a clip across the ear with a bunch of keys.

Sheila White remembers Father Breen,

He was a very well-respected priest. Everyone loved him, he was a very handsome man. He could have been a film star really. I think a lot of the ladies liked the looks of him but he had a beautiful speaking voice and he was a very nice man.

George Street Bar with church through arch

Life could sometimes be difficult for catholics as Mike Race explains,

I desperately wanted to be a cub but there wasn't a catholic troop, so I went to St Margaret's. The second time, they asked me about the oath, I remember telling the leader I was a catholic, and he said, 'I'm sorry, you can't join'. Can't give an allegiance to the Queen evidently, with being a catholic.

But there were compensations at the new boys' secondary school, which had opened at the corner of Margaret Street and Walmgate after the war,

They had competitions in the various groups, to collect for masses for the dead and put these graphs on the board, of which group had given the most, and always our group, the De La Salle, had given about three times more than anybody else. And that was because my mother used to always give me about half a crown.

Being an altar boy I helped the priest with funerals. And if there was one on during the week when I was at school, I'd get a call from the church to go. I didn't mind that because you'd get out of school for an hour, attend the church service, say the responses, get a ride out in a car to the cemetery, wave the incense about and watch the priest put soil on the grave, then get tenpence before you got back to school, go to the shop and buy some liquorice.

St George's Church altar boys c1950
Back left, Father Moynagh; right, Father Breen

I remember once we were in the schoolyard and a child had died at a house on the corner of Margaret Street. This woman was inviting all the boys in to view this baby who had died. It was on the back kitchen table in a little box, tidied and seen

to by the undertaker. Of course, all the boys were absolutely fascinated, first time they'd seen a dead body.

Tom Rhodes went to St George's,

One Friday I went, and on the Thursday I was off in the cattle market as usual and she'd took the class round the Minster. Friday morning there wasn't only me got the cane, there was one or two more, they knew where we'd been. They had to challenge us 'cos we was registered missing. Then she said, 'Right you all enjoyed yourselves yesterday round the Minster, I want you to write a nice composition about it'. I thought, 'I'll have to put summat', so I wrote down, 'The Minster is a big building, it's in York somewhere. A fella came along one day with a handcart and put a window in, another day somebody else came and they were handling some stones and they were putting these stones near t'Minster and there was a joiner came.' And Monday morning she'd collected the papers. Then, 'I'll read the best, oh no I won't I'll read the worst'. I said, 'I wonder who it is' and bloody hell, it was mine. And she shouted, 'Rhodes, come out' and I stood at side of her. I was best ducker and dodger in t'school, 'cos you're last out, you used to sidestep like a boxer. Of course they all grinned and laughed, and I thought, 'You right prats, wait while tomorrow, I'll have you', 'cos there was some sweet boys but I was rough and I didn't care.

David Wilde, who taught at the school, remembers its reputation for toughness,

If you'd been at St George's, you either turned out a villain or a policeman. The school supplied lots of rugby league players, the best in the area.

The last chapter in the history of St George's Secondary School took place in September 1996 with its demolition. The buildings had become derelict and were being used by squatters. A new development costing £1.3 million is to be built on the site, with 36 one-bedroomed flats as housing for single people within the city. The opening is planned for summer 1997.

The parish was a very vigorous place, with a ceilidh each weekend during the 1950s and 1960s. Men and women came along to dance the

Pride of Erin, the Siege of Ennis, and other Irish country dances. The school hall was always crowded out.

Terry Kilmartin was involved with St George's youth/social club which operated in the basement of the old St George's boys' school which was directly behind the church,

From twelve year old I used to look after the billiard table, then when I was 18 I was put on the committee. We had modern dancing, ceilidh dancing, rambles, fancy dress, anything you can imagine, we had it.

When we got started I used to teach judo and self-defence. And we had a great atmosphere and what happened was that in the top of the building they got dry rot and the Inspector come one day and he says, 'This is dangerous'. Downstairs, they used it during the week for a canteen for St George's, both schools. So they had to seal the top off, and it closed the club.

St George's School winners of Intermediate Cricket Cup 1951
Back row: M race, Jackson, ?, Phil Scott, Bainbridge, Raftery
Front row: Goodwin, Mellor, Ellis, Hattee, Coughlin

Brian Fletcher became leader of the club from 1950 to 1962,

Once people reached the age of 14 they could join. Terry Kilmartin and Mick Donaghue was involved in running it. There were some non-catholics, but I was one of the very few. I think there were about three.

One of the highlights in those days was the Sunday evening sixpenny dance, which Alf and Mrs Bardy ran. In the week it was table tennis, snooker and a canteen. Branched out into netball and rounders teams, cricket and football teams. I got involved through the youth service.

St George's Youth Club outing 1950s

Mike Race also belonged to the club,

When I used to go in the 50's that was in the era of what we called 'bopping'. They used to dance with these thick creepers on and everybody used to be doing this jivin' and Mick Rogers'd rush in and say, 'We're havin' none of that bobbing'. I used to think it would have been nice to have had the basement as a club, it would have made a super little club - like the Cavern.

26

St George's Youth Club football team c1955
Mike Race far left, back row

Brian continues,

We were open every night. Sunday lunch time it was the youth club, Sunday night was officially only open for the dance and the only record player was downstairs. There was a canteen where you could get tea and biscuits, snacks, crisps and wagon wheels. The membership varied from 20 to 80 or 90 at one time.

In 1956 the social club started collecting weekly to go to Lourdes for '58, which was the centenary year. People were paying 6d a week, to save up for the fare, that was Whitsun '58 when the parish went as a parish. They went again in 1959 and '60. One year we had a private plane!

The dark television room. That's where all the romances started. We used to close at 10 o' clock but if there was things like showjumping that went on 'til midnight!

When the clearances occurred and whole communities were split and moved to various parts of York, each catholic group had a new church built. St Aelred's catholic church in Fifth Avenue, Tang Hall, recently celebrated its 40th anniversary with a mass which attracted a congregation of nearly 800. There are also St Joseph's in Kingsway North, Church of our Lady down Thanet Road, and St Paulinus in Bell Farm.

As well as the established churches, there have also been a few non-conformist establishments. On 6th May 1908, the Salvation Army established a corps in Harper's Yard, off Walmgate. It was known locally as the 'vineyard'. By the First World War it had closed, and was later relocated in Acomb. During this period, the Army band marched through Layerthorpe, Hungate and Walmgate and suffered not merely verbal harassment, but 'a plentiful supply of horse-droppings provided handy missiles for the mischievous'.

The Quakers started a boys' mission school in Hope Street in 1828, which lasted until 1890. Attendance averaged over 50 in the first year and by 1856, 860 youths and 25 men had passed through the school. There was also a library and a savings bank, with opportunities for gardening. The weekly programme offered,

Sunday 8.30	Breakfast for the unemployed
9-10	Men's class
3-4	Women's class
6.30 - 8	Children's service
Monday	Sewing meeting
Tuesday	Children's choir practice
Wednesday	Band of Hope and educational class for men
Thursday	Boys' club
Friday	Football club

Billiards available from 6.30 to 10 pm each night.

3

The Struggle to Survive

For most people in Walmgate, life was sometimes little more than a matter of survival. It was not a question of finding new and different ways of entertainment, but rather of keeping their families clothed and fed. In the 19th century, life was particularly grim, with appalling housing conditions in this area. Even in the 1920s, one in ten children never reached their first birthday. Poverty was a serious reality, and this continued right through the depression of the 1930s.

Kenneth Barton's mother worked in the early 1930s on a food programme,

York Corporation started meals for necessitous children and one of the first projects was in St Margaret's Church hall in Walmgate. This was next door, up a passage, to Kilmartin's lodging-house. My mother was employed to feed these children. She had two assistants.

The children were from the unemployed and, of course, not very healthy. Under-nourished. Produce was obtained from local retailers, under contract to supply food. There were three long tables with approximately 25 to 30 children each side. The plates were put out and food served and passed along. Children are cute and if it was a big lad at the end of the table, he would put the plate on his knee and take another, so he got two helpings. Knives, forks and spoons were laid out and it was found that the children would use the knives for warring with each other so they had to be taken off the tables.

They had mincemeat, mashed potato, cabbage, cauliflowers, sprouts, cooked on three gas cookers. Spotted dick puddings, rhubarb and custard, or rice pudding with sultanas on top.

Some of the boys were mischievous and my mother used to tell them to wait outside. She didn't turn any of them away or make them do without. If mother couldn't control them, she would tell me to jump out the window, if they stood in the doorway, and go to the policeman that was on point duty at Walmgate Bar. That quietened down the situation.

They did have a run of rats, and my mother had to put a pan of water on to boil and then throw it over the rats as they came in because they were very determined.

She worked until she was 60, doing this type of work. It was a success, and further meals were put on the curriculum. They started feeding expectant mothers because they were not very strong and they were given a high tea, from three o'clock until four in the afternoon.

Conditions in the Area

Dick Calpin remembers conditions in his house in Rosemary Yard, which was owned by Leethams,

They wouldn't do any repairs at all. We was damp and when we used to go out at night-time and then put the light on, the beetles would be running out of all corners. There was one tap in the yard for six families. When it was winter we had to muffle it up to keep the frost out. There was no electricity, we had one of those paraffin lamps. Our bed was on the floor.

He also explains that people would help out their neighbours by lending rugs and carpets to those who were having visitors, just to improve their homes.

Ray D recalls the area,

Man alive, it was rough. If you kept a dog under the same conditions as what we was kept under as kids, you'd be pinched. Certainly was dreadful. No water in the houses, no lighting, no toilets, and if you had anything to eat you were a very lucky lad. That's no exaggeration. But if anybody had nothing to eat, somebody'd give you something. I lost me mother before I was a year old. Me father brought me up so I had a lot of sympathy from the grandmothers in the area.

Mrs Mary Jeffrey lived in Chapel Row,

In that yard there was ten houses. We had a family of ten and we had one down and two up and we had four taps outside and the last house had a tremendous big family. In our house there was me mother and father in one bed and I had a sister, we used to sleep in a little single bed in the same room, me three elder brothers slept in one bed in the back room, I don't know where the rest slept. Me mother'd be married when she was 21 and she was 45 when she died, a month after me youngest brother was born.

You never thought any better of anybody else, because everybody was poor. It's after the war that things changed, people working made up their mind that their children weren't going to have the same life as what they had.

Thomas Abbot remembers the effects of the First World War,

You saw men in a terrible state. They just existed in lodging-houses and some had no legs, just stumps, leather aprons on the end so they could shuffle along.

One old boy, I think the way he turned out that he must have been an officer. He'd got an old suit on which was immaculate in a way but well worn. He allus wore spats, allus had his rolled umbrella, his bowler hat, his overcoat, a dress coat it was. He'd got a regular route, he used to go to the Cenotaph, and all of a sudden, he was walking, thinking he was among a lot of shellbursts, the way he used to react.

And he used to stop and salute and he carried himself well and somehow even as a kid, I had a lot of respect for him. These men used to be gradually fading away, used to just die off in the lodging-houses, nobody could care less. I was born in 1919, and these chaps were all floating around and of course Walmgate was a place they went. Some of them had got crutches but most hadn't, they had wooden legs. It had its effects on me.

There was one who used to sit there all day, and all he had was laces and boxes of matches and he used to sell them. That's how he got the money to pay for his lodgings that night.

Noel Attree explains,

Those ladies amazed me, when I think back. I knew most of the yards, right up to Walmgate Bar, 'cos you're always playing with young lads of your own age. There's always these ladies with anything from one to fifteen kids. And then more often than not, in the Windsor chair you'd see somebody there, a man or a woman, very elderly. In wintertime, again the fire, you'd have the cape round them or a shawl.

She'd time to care for a person like that, with all that family to see to, and keep the house clean. It was only two up, two down, but imagine what a state it must have been in. I've seen those ladies with the pottery mould. The step outside, they'd scrub it till it nearly shone. The windowsills and the windows were always spotless.

Then they used to do the baking. Big earthenware bowls, the doings in there with a lovely white cover over, waiting for the bread to rise. They'd take it out and knock lumps out of it. Must have had arms like Popeye, with what they used to do.

Some of them coughing their heads off with TB, the woman wringing her hands and wondering whether she was going to be alive next year. And wondering how she was going to manage. I think a fella went out for a drink to get a bit of relief from it all.

Betty Thompson recounts stories from her mother's childhood,

My mother was an angel and she was only four foot eleven, but she had a very hard life of it. She had a little brother, he died of whooping cough, he was only two years old, another one was killed in the war but the other eight lived. People lived in constant fear, old wives tales that they used to pass on were very good but a lot of people died having babies. She knew a woman and she wasn't a qualified midwife or anything, she just used to go around with a jar of vaseline delivering for these people. They used to scream. Women would take powdered steel for unwanted pregnancies. They'd take anything, just swallowed it. They were so frightened, there was no birth control in them days. There was no food to feed them, they couldn't afford it.

Henry King remembers the soup kitchen,

Where kids could go with a penny and get a bowl o'soup, there was a big boiler to keep the stuff in. You could get a pennorth o'soup with celery and carrots and turnips in it. This was in the thirties.

Joyce Burnett remembers,

Half an egg, that's what we had. And my Dad used to do toasted cheese. He used to put milk in and we had the gravy, we didn't have the cheese. I can remember my mother saying, 'You've got the goodness in the gravy, get that down you'. You had margarine, but butter was for them that's working.

Ina Paterson recalls,

You went down to the market and bought your week's supply of fresh fruit and veg. Everybody had a pantry and a stone shelf and me mother had a meat safe, a little wooden cupboard on little legs and three sides of it were covered with a fine gauze so it let the air in to keep it cool. And milk in those days, no fridges, you had a bucket of cold water and you kept topping it up from the tap and stood your milk bottles in.

Near St George's School is, I remember going as a young child to one of those cottages with my mother. We went in to see Granny Scales and she was related somehow, a widow and getting on a bit. She kept a lot of children in her care that were left with her day by day or week by week. They always called 'em 'nussbairns' and she looked after 'em like a foster mother would now. But she did it to earn a little bit of money, and the girls either had them as illegitimate, which was a great scandal, they kept it quiet, or they were perhaps born to mothers who'd lost their husbands. In that cottage you stepped down and the floor was on two levels. There was these children, she used to have mebbe about nine or ten, of various ages.

School Street, Navigation Road street party 1918

Mary Dent was a visitor for Macmillans Cancer relief during the Second World War,

I used to visit some of the really dreadful places, just an up and a down. You walked in and there was just a room above, that's where the patient lived. Some of them were pretty grim. You could go into the house next door and it was like a little palace. It would be beautiful, it was just the difference in the people. The children were neglected but the man had to have the best. It was, 'Keep the man happy', he had to have his beer. I finished visiting in '77 but it was always the same. 'He has to have his beer at the weekend then he vomits on a Monday with all the bile'.

Mary Booker would help her neighbour,

I used to go for this old lady's medicine, and she had loads of cats, she was about ninety. Me mam used to say to me, 'Go clean up for poor Bessie'. She had a bed downstairs and a table and she used to say, 'Gerrunder that bed' and she'd give me a bucket of water, carbolic soap and a scrubbing brush and I used to put me hand in, loads of cat muck.

Down t'back there was six toilets. They used to get overflowing. They didn't know much about plumbing in those days. This sixth house, the woman that lived there had a great big lock and key on it and we'd say, 'Please can we use your toilet?' 'No, you can't, if I start letting you have it, everybody else'll want it'. In the next street, there was an old lady sat there, all in black and she used to have a clay pipe. By her house there was eight toilets. She used to say, 'Come on, go in there'.

The old women used to row like the divil with their husbands. One woman'd been rowing with her husband and she threw herself in the river. By t'time anybody knew, she was well under and they couldn't find her. Me dad went down with me and he got a little boat and a grappling hook and he went down the river where t'grass was and he stuck this thing in her corsets and dragged her out. He took his trilby off and put it on her face and took his coat and put it over her, and he got commended in the Press.

My brother was right poorly. He was six and he started school and I took him and I had him by the hand and he kept saying, 'I'm right cold'. I said to me mam, 'Let Sonny sit by the fire because he's cold' and he said, 'Me belly hurts' and so she said, 'We'll put you to bed'. And he was dead and buried in a week. He had double pneumonia.

Rubye Readhead remembers Hotham's Court,

This lady had brick floors, with no coverings on them, and a deal table, an old copper that she washed in. She had a fire oven and everything was done in that. And she always wore a black dress, a big white apron, and a little black hard hat, like a bowler. The thing I remember most was how spartan her house was, but how hard she worked. One of her daughters-in-law had died very young, leaving two small children, and they were brought up by their grandmother. We used to call for them to come out and play and you never saw her sitting down, always working, baking, washing, cooking meals.

In the courtyard in Chapel Row there was a family who lived in a one-up and one-down. The mother had just had another baby and there was already about four of them. Our neighbour came in and told my mother about the baby, and said, 'She's got nothing for that child to wear'. So they scrummaged around and got all sorts of bits and pieces. The bedroom was only big enough for the double bed and a chest of drawers and I think there was a chair. The woman was in bed with this baby and they pulled a drawer out of the chest, and lined it with pieces of blanket they'd brought and sheeting. My first insight into what poverty was really like.

The Children of Walmgate

Frederick Atkinson remembers children in the cattle market,

When they were doing Paragon Street, there used to be night watchman with a brazier and youngsters used to lay round that all night long to keep warm. They were a grand lot of kids but they were starved to death, they used to even go and get condensed milk tins out of ashbins, and go into cattle market and lean through railings and milk cows and drink that. They were really hungry was them youngsters.

Owen Calpin recalls,

We all turned to crime, we didn't call it crime, we called it existence. As kids we often used to go raiding the stalls in the market. We could run from one end of Parliament Street to the other, grab what we wanted and they were shouting and screaming behind us but they couldn't catch us, too many for a start off. We had nothing, nothing at all.

We never left Walmgate as kids, we never went into hotels or big houses, every house we visited was exactly t'same as ours. I can remember one trip. There was a fella called Forster-Todd, [he was Lord Mayor], and he organised a poor children's outing to Filey. There was buses lined up in the cattle market right up to Foss Islands, absolutely full of kids. I can see 'em now crawling up Garrowby Hill and the first time they'd seen the sea.

Joyce Burnett also recalls a tragic incident from her childhood,

Our house in Clock Yard was right at bottom on the left-hand side and there was a hole in the fence there. There was a family called Morrisons and the little boy was my friend. I was with him all the time. And me and him went through this fence, which we were always told not to do. And when they were looking for us

36

they knew where to look, where we weren't supposed to be. This certain day, we both fell in, he was swept away and I hung on to the reeds. And I always remember all the women was running through this hole in the fence. Course they got me out but he was drowned. And I'm frightened of water wherever I go.

The incident took place in June 1932, when Douglas Morrison of 64a Walmgate, aged five, had gone out to play and fell into the Foss. Three policemen and five civilians in swimming costumes were helped by a man in a boat in a brave attempt to rescue the little boy, but it was all in vain.

There was very little money and some children had to work from a young age to help with the family finances. Stan Cowen, for example, became an errand lad for a butcher's shop next to the Five Lions, called Gaythorpe's,

I used to work on a Friday night about half past five to half past eight, and on a Saturday from half past eight in the morning to gone nine. I was eleven years of age and my first job on a Saturday morning was to take down the shutters. The man I worked for used to take snuff. And I'd go to the shop for his snuff and for tobacco. You could get the flake tobacco loose, but mostly it was in like coils of rope. And he would have on the counter a small wooden block like a cheese slicer, with a knife on it and a blade. And he'd cut a slice of what they called thin twist or thick twist.

Owen Calpin was even younger,

I started work when I was nine year old. One of me uncles used to have horse and cart and in the market they'd bring the stalls in on a Friday morning and erect 'em. On Saturday night they had to be taken down and I went with him. I'd get a big bar of chocolate or summat. When I was ten I worked all day Saturday on horse and cart with a fella from Dunnington and we went round James Street and Bishopthorpe Road selling vegetables. He used to give me a shilling. When I was eleven, I was working nights and Saturdays.

Stan Lea remembers potato picking,

In October when the potato was ready, they used to go to the Bar to be picked up. He used to pick up eighteen, they was working in three gangs, three sixes in rows. All the kids used to congregate there with their packing-up, for the first day when it started. It was a week off school.

Hill's Yard with boat 1933

Violet Quigley recalls,

Mebbe me mam would be baking and she'd put too much water in, she used to say to me, 'Go and ask Mrs Murray to lend me a dash of flour, I've drowned the miller.' One thing they would never lend was salt. It was supposed to be unlucky. But anything else, if they had it, you could have a dash of it. When anybody was having a baby, they was there all t'time, helping 'em. I remember my mam, she was up all night with Mary Calpin when she had a baby, then she went tatie picking next morning, she didn't go to bed at all. Up Fulford it was, they used to walk there. I once went with her, I must have only been about 13, and all t'old Irish women used to go. With me being young I was miles in front of 'em, and

*they all started playing war with me. We thought we was millionaires that week
'cos we got ten shilling a day, me mam's five shilling and mine.*

The Second World War

Rubye Readhead from George Street remembers,

*During the war they had a canteen for the forces and mother used to go and help
there. And they were asked if any serviceman that was lonely or feeling homesick,
would they invite them to their homes. Ours was open house and these chaps
used to come down. What they loved to do was to make toast on the open fire.
Toast with jam. And they used to help my younger sister with her homework,
and if they were there when she was washing her hair, they used to love to help
dry it. I suppose it reminded them of their own children. My brother was in the
Royal Artillery at Spurn Point, and he used to bring his friends home. So we had
some very interesting parties. One night we went through the floorboards in the
front room, because of their army boots, and their dancing.*

Terry Kilmartin recalls,

*They bombed Hope Street. We was all in t'shelters wi't Calpins and all singing in
there and they come down and frightened us to death. They machine-gunned it
and they dropped the bomb which went right in front of the Brown Cow. It
knocked two houses down and if you look at Brown Cow you'll see new bricks,
that's where me uncle John patched it up. At the bottom I picked up a piece of
shrapnel and burnt me hand and it was about a foot long. In the cattle market, all
the bodies during that raid, was put in there where t'cows used to be. I saw 'em all
and it was a very frightening experience. It bonded everybody together in t'street
and we all looked after each other.*

In 1947 York had terrible floods. Ina Paterson recalls,

*I was at work at the time, used to cycle down from Hull Road, straight through
Walmgate and round Merchantgate. That particular day there'd been an awful lot
of snow, it was a really bad winter and it was about March time, and the snow
was so deep, and when all that was melting it caused tremendous floods, all
across near the Red Lion where it dips down slightly. And they had horses and*

carts, which were quite common even then in the 40s, and they used to put us on with the bikes and trundle us through the flood water, which was quite deep and you couldn't walk through it very well.

Maureen Aspinall also experienced the floods,

I lived upstairs for a week. They used to come in a rowboat and bring us our food. The water came up through the drains. It was six steps up and I stepped onto it and went crashing down into a blooming great sea of water, and I'm screaming. Me mother come down and me dad, 'Where's all the water coming from?' I can see the rowboat coming down, and we're all hanging out o't'window and they come and put ladder up and they brought us tea.

I thought, 'Oh lovely I've missed all this school and exams' and I went back the following week and they put me in a room by meself to do these exams!

Criterion Cocoa Works

4

Working Walmgate

Walmgate was certainly a hive of industry. From the late 18th to the early 20th century, it was the scene of almost every kind of manufacturers. A lead mill, cotton manufacturer's, cocoa works and woollen warehouse rubbed shoulders with Bellerby's match mill (specialising in many varieties, such as Rangoon, Coral and Peabody matches), a plane and tool manufacturers, (George Eastwood's, which won first prize at the Great Exhibition in 1851), artificial manure manufacturers, looking-glass manufacturers, bonecrushers and rape dust dealers, provision merchants, and the steam marble works.

Piccadilly, then only a small street off Walmgate, was also buzzing. In 1880 the Ebor Cigar Works was very popular. The owner, Oldfield Marshall, advertised a variety of brands, which ranged from the familiar Havanas and Manila cheroots, to the more exotically named Great Northerns, Pilots, Dreadnoughts and 'the celebrated Dandy Dyndmonts'.

Small businesses really flourished in the period before the 1970s when big companies started their takeover bids. The area was alive with small shops of every kind, where almost anything was available, from cars and hi-fi equipment, to quality fruit and vegetables. Craftsmen thrived in the area, where jewellers, watchmakers, and fashion emporiums could be spotted beside innumerable food stores, carpet showrooms, and second-hand furniture shops. Independent Chapel Yard, behind 54a Walmgate, once had a weaver called John Major. Among the more unusual places over the years have been the canine beauty salon, the rubber stamp shop, the party and novelty store and Bamboo Grove, which specialised in Oriental crafts.

The cattle market was just through the bar and drew on the Walmgate population for its workers. Poad's seed merchants, the Navigation Road glassworks and the brewery off George Street were all busy. By the 1950s, much of Navigation was just waste ground, where children played, sometimes coming across bits of coloured glass. When Herbert Todd's electrical shop was built about 1972, the foundations were dug and the old yellow brick wind tunnels from the glass factory were discovered, ten feet down. Today there are few examples of industry in the district. The Yorkshire Evening Press is the last company in York to use barges for its deliveries, but other skilled workers can still be found in the street, like the clockmaker, picture-framers and pine shop.

One occupation particularly associated with Walmgate is that of pipe-making. The Shaftoe family ran a profitable business in Barleycorn Yard from 1814. They specialised in clay tobacco pipes, a great favourite with the Irish community. The York Archaeological Trust has a dig in the garden of Ellerkers, and various objects, or 'small finds' have been discovered during the last two years, including a number of these pipes. George Shaftoe, one of the last of the family to be involved in the business, died in 1846 and was buried in the same graveyard as Dick Turpin. After that, the family branched off into other areas, including stonemasonry. Another yard further along Walmgate became known as Shaftoe's Yard, as the family rented out property to local inhabitants.

Thomlinson-Walker

The Victoria Ironworks in Walmgate was the site of John Walker's ironfounders, engineers and whitesmiths. Walker had been in business since the beginning of the 19th century, and his first great commission was to build the gates of Kew Gardens in London. After his death in 1853, he was succeeded by his son William, who took his mother's maiden name of Thomlinson and added it to his own surname. In 1871, he had 62 employees and was receiving iron by barge on the Foss. Ten years later the foundry was extended. Thomlinson-Walker designed and built the ironwork for many York buildings, including chapels, banks and private residences. He built the gates of the Royal Botanical Gardens in Mauritius, as well as the railings outside the British Museum in London. He also manufactured iron fences, stoves, iron and brass bedsteads, pig troughs, mangles, washing machines, ovens and boilers.

Thomlinson-Walker

For many years in the 1950s and '60s, Navigation Road was home to a fleet of bow-top Romany caravans which were very ornate and beautifully painted, and mostly made in Leeds.

Ray D remembers,

One of the families was called Dear. This man could not read or write, but he could build these bow tops magnificently, he used to make the wheels, the shafts, the tops and paint them. Very very skilled man.

Alfred Chapman's cabinet manufacturer's and sawmill factory in Lord Nelson Yard, advertising in 1884, later became the Criterion Cocoa Works, and the Gazette in May 1912 reported that the Corporation was to purchase the works in connection with the construction of a new street from Pavement to Piccadilly.

Walmgate was also home to a small Italian community, including the Betchettis, plaster figure-makers living in Margaret Street. The Rossettis from Navigation Road, the Almonio family of Hope Street and the

Recchia family were all ice-cream manufacturers. The latter family lived in a passage off Long Close Lane, and would go round the streets selling, often accompanied by a barrel organ. Frankie's ice-cream parlour was situated at 158 Walmgate. The son of the family, Private Dorril Frankie of the Northumberland Fusiliers, was killed in action in 1916.

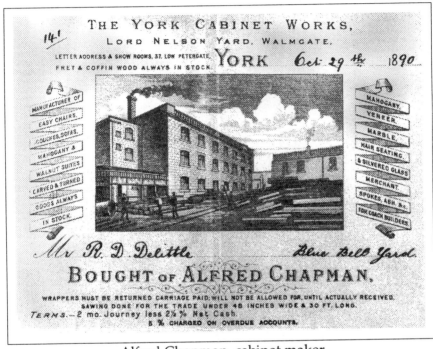

Alfred Chapman, cabinet maker

Sheila White remembers going across to Frankie's for ice-cream. He used to have a dancing bear chained outside his shop.

Terry Kilmartin recalls,

There was the ice-cream people in Long Close Lane. The pony went into the front room and its head used to be through into the lane and they used to push the cart on its side to go down the passage, it wouldn't go t'other way.

Isaac Poad's

Poad's of Walmgate was an international firm of grain and seed merchants. They also won many prizes for their potatoes, which boasted such interesting names as Eldorado, Royal Kidney, Empress Queen, Evergood, Northern Star and Sir John Llewellyn. The Eldorados were sold at Smithfield Show for £600, an average of £25 per tuber!

Arthur Brown, Director of Poad's

Arthur Brown worked there from 1929 when he joined the firm as a junior, until he retired in 1980,

I took control when my late chairman, Mark Cockerill, died in 1954. I was the youngest director, and I developed the grain side. Poads became very well known in the malting, brewing and distilling industry. In 1980 I said, 'That's it,' except any big financial decisions and the last one I made was to accept the third offer of the Yorkshire Evening Press for the premises in Walmgate, built in 1893. The business is now in Cattal.

Isaac Poad

It was actually the other side of Hurst's Yard until the Corporation were laying new drains down Walmgate and the foundation sank so Isaac Poad moved across the yard and sued the Corporation - and won! I think the reason they went into

PRICE LIST ON APPLICATION.

Seed Potato Catalogue, 1904.

ISAAC POAD & SONS,

CORN, SEED AND POTATO MERCHANTS,

84 and 86, Walmgate,

YORK.

Telegraphic Address:
" POAD, YORK."

National Telephone :
32.

Poad's of Walmgate

Walmgate was because of the old cattle market. It was a busy sort of business street.

We used to do a lot of growing, in fact Poads had three farms in Yorkshire. Isaac Poad used to go down to London every Monday to attend the grain market which I carried on many years later. I had a buying permit on London Corn Exchange, bought barley. I also bought in Norfolk, Suffolk, Essex, Lincolnshire and the Border counties. Before the war we used to import a lot of barley from Denmark. In 1937 it was the biggest importation of foreign grain the firm had ever had and funnily enough, that was the year I took over as manager of the grain side.

Irish women in potato fields

We used to go to Leeds by rail and there was a chap with a hand cart, we had sample bags. Now it's packets, but you'd big heavy leather Gladstone bags and you used to chuck 'em on this handcart and take 'em from the station to the Leeds Corn Exchange.

You had to wear a suit and tie, and a trilby hat. But Mark Cockerill used to wear those stiff collars. When I first went to Poad's, one of my jobs was to take his *collars to the Chinese laundry. And I used to get his library books from Bilsbrough's in Parliament Street, he was a member of their private library.*

Isaac Poad was on the original council of the first National Association of Corn and Agricultural merchants and I was honoured in 1968 to be its president. We had Poad's originally and we finished up with four companies, and covered the whole field of agriculture.

We sold animal feeds, manure, clover, grass and root seeds to farmers, and we bought the grain from them. We sold to millers, maltsters, breweries. Every brewery doesn't malt their own barley, they buy barley from the wholesale maltsters, and also distillers, we have a big distilling trade. I enjoyed it all.

The photograph on the previous page shows labourers at work picking potatoes for Poad's. Most of these women would be Irish.

Cow wallopers at Walmgate Bar

The Cattle Market

A cattle market stood in this area from the 16th century when a charter was granted for buying and selling cattle, horses and sheep. Originally it was sited in Walmgate itself, within the walls, and the Long Close, a field beside the bar, was where the cattle rested. Long Close Lane was built on the field in 1810. Before the market was contained outside the bar, the cattle were sold in the streets.

The cattle market building with its twin cupolas, was built in 1826. In 1843 it was described as having 44 pens, with accommodation for 616 fat cattle, some lean cattle and 6,750 sheep! It continued for almost 150 years, until the final trading day on 25th February 1971. The building was demolished in 1976 and the market moved out of the city to Murton. The Barbican centre stands on the old site. At the end of the 19th century there was also a cattle spice mill in Navigation Road, run by T. Myers. In advertising his spices at twenty-one shillings a hundred-weight, Mr Myers boasted that he had 'acquired an European reputation' and even went so far as to state that he 'challenges the world to compete with him'.

Walmgate Bar with sheep

Horse fair at cattle market

Henry King remembers the cattle market, because he worked for a city centre shop which operated two stalls there,

One was just near to the back entrance to the City Arms Hotel. The farmers seemed to stick to the City Arms, and all the cattle drovers and bullock wallopers went to the other places.

From George Street to Walmgate Bar on t'main road, there was little offices, the Midland Bank had one, it was only open when there was anything on t'market. And there was another chap that sold ropes and binder twine.

In September there was the sheep sales, and the fatstock show in December. I had to be there at eight o'clock in t'morning setting stall out. You took your dinner and I was quite happy. And if boss came and relieved me, I could go and have a walk round. All these other people had stalls there. I used to go and get me dinner free on some o't'stalls, because they had a place at back where they could interview people that were buying their stuff. I could get in there and get a few sandwiches and a pint o'beer. They had gallons of beer in these stalls on racks at the back, it

51

was all to get trade. You'd get invited in, you just put your glass under t'tap and helped yourself.

All the farmers were drunk and some of these farmers even then were very well off although it was a depressed time. We sold Lord Hamlet cigars and they were eight pence and they'd come and buy one cigar. And we sold Criterion, about ten pence each and they'd buy a cedar box of fifty to take home. In the market there was a horse drawn coffee stall. He had an urn on the counter with a gas flame under it. He sold marvellous pork pies and you could have a steak and kidney pie hot. They always seemed to taste better on a cold day in t'cattle market than they did at home.

Branch Line

The Foss Islands branch line carried traffic from December 1879 (twenty six years after the Island was drained to create Foss Islands Road) to Autumn 1988. At one time the depot supplied sand to the glassworks, and there were sidings into the electricity power station. The cattle market docks were here. The railway had rulleys (heavy duty carts pulled by horses) to distribute goods from the station to various parts of York. These were later replaced by three wheeler electric vehicles (mini articulated lorries). The Evening Press of May 1880 had an advertisement for a dwelling house, shop and warehouse in the stretch of houses known as Walmgate Bar Within. The premises were described as being 'in close proximity to the new railway station', which would be the branch line established the previous year.

Violet Quigley recalls,

We used to go in the cattle market when they were selling, especially to hear t'auctioneer, way he used to talk. T'lads and fellas used to go in and milk cows, and come away with a big bucket of milk. That's what amuses me, we used to drink it, the mothers used to make puddings with it. And it was pure milk.

Eileen Holgate 1930s

Eileen Brown was the daughter of Len Holgate, a self-employed cattle haulage remover. He had the first motorised cattle vehicle in York,

Me dad had all the pub yards with horses, pigs, donkeys, ponies, goats, anything and everything, And we'd rent nearly all the pub yards in the area for this livestock. 'Cos they nearly all had stabling at the back.

Me dad never worked for anybody but hisself. He would go round when they got any livestock, Wrights the big butchering firm or anybody and he'd mark the cattle what they wanted moving, and he would move them all to various slaughterhouses. There was Dents, Frears and Ellerkers but me dad moved stuff

Len Holgate and sister

for all and sundry. I used to have an old bicycle and go and collect the money and it was about three and six a time then. There was fatstock market on a Monday and store market on a Thursday and the cattle used to come in from Ireland to the cattle docks, and there was hundreds of them and all the drovers there with their sticks whacking 'em. And they used to walk them right to Osbaldwick, and they broke into everybody's garden as they were going along, these cattle, everybody went mad and then next morning they had to bring them back into York because the cattle market was right along the bar walls right down to Fishergate. If people bought them they took them to the farms to fatten for Irish beef.

They'd travelled overnight from Holyhead so they took them up to this layerage and it was what you call Corporation Farm and they were able to rest overnight. They were watered and if any were lame they had to be shot. We lived in a house where we could look over and see them unloading all these wagons. And if they had to be shot they brought the knacker man along with the gun, put it at the animal's head, and with one shot it was dead.

My husband went to work for me father and somebody come to tell me dad that they had a bull that'd gone mad and it was in the pens. My husband had to get up on a beam, and drop a rope on its head to choke it, got its head and fastened it down. But it was a mad bull, definitely mad.

My father kept Walmgate Bar stood up. Because that was where people knew he would be if they wanted him. And he was the cleanest man you ever saw in your life. If he come in five times a day, which we only lived on Foss Islands Road then, he changed his boots every time he came in. He took them off, he washed the cow muck off them and let them dry, and he had a pair that he'd cleaned with Tonett boot polish and they went on. And he was such a big man that he had his boots made for him. They were made by somebody at Newmarket. They used to send us three pieces of leather for what colour he wanted to choose. Everybody knew me dad by his brown boots. He had his caps made for him at Dunns. They sent us material and he chose it. He had his suits made for him. He couldn't wear a shirt because you couldn't get one to fit him. He'd got one with the old-fashioned neck and he wore a great big lovely, gypsy silk, that he put on his knee and folded it like a baby's nappy then rolled it back and put that round his neck and he tied it in a knot twice.

I love smell of animals and manure. Give me a cow-house when they're empty and it's buzzing with thousands of flies and I'm happy. And my daughter Glenys, she died young, loved the market and me dad loved our Glenys. A great big man and a little girl and you saw 'em on horse and cart. We went in the market and we used to go up in the ring where they were auctioning, and down below she saw Grandpa and waved to him. And there was Jack Craft's coffee stall and me dad used to bring us a cup of coffee up there. Oh yes we were allus in t'cattle market. I loved it.

Me dad got this Model T-Ford. We were moving up then. You didn't earn a lot of money those days but we were never poor in the meaning that people were poor, because me mother was a dressmaker as well.

Geese ran from the Waggon and Horses yard, with a smooth-haired sheepdog. People wanted a goose and they'd say, 'Will you have owt on for Christmas, Len?' and me dad fed them up and sold them, with the feathers and everything on. You never used to pluck your geese those days, but you clipped their wings so that they couldn't fly away.

Walmgate before the First World War

Stan Cowen recalls the deals made by farmers,

Round the Cattle Market Inn which was at the other end, there was maybe 20 or 30 in that pen and there was an interested buyer, he wouldn't go in the pen to look at them, they would open the pen door and drive the cattle out and they'd be milling around in that little bit of road while the buyer just sized them up. And you could always tell when they was going to strike a deal because they'd hold a hand out and if the other person was going to make an agreement, he'd spit on his hand and then that was it. It was as good as a signature.

Tom Rhodes helped out,

I had a little stick, about two foot, and on Thursday morning, I used to go in t'cattle market. There weren't only me, there were four or five lads. The drovers used to bring the cattle in from up Hull Road, different fields out of Osbaldwick and all round there. The dealer, that was like the servant of Irish breeders, he was in charge and he'd rent two or three pens according to how many cattle was coming over. Some of the farmers'd have a look and they'd turn the cattle out of the pens and be feeling around. They knew what they were buying. I was watching, never saying owt just watching, and when they bought they allus used to hit their hand, and that bargain was kept. Then I'd dash up, 'Do you want help with 'em sir?' 'Well I'm going a fair way.' 'Dun't matter sir, I can walk and it's all right'. And there was thirty cattle. They'd be two or three year old beasts, fairly thin, 'cos they was sold off and I used to be at the back walking. I've walked to Stamford Bridge and all over sometimes. There were no cattle trucks in them days so you had to walk with them. There was no cars about, you were safe walking, and when we got to the farm, the missis give me a good meal, and then a blanket, and I used to have to sleep in t'hayplace. I never got in the house properly, I got in the part with the workmen. And next morning she give me a good breakfast and a shilling and I used to set off back home.

And I went into school, 'Right, Rhodes where was you yesterday?' Course it was always, 'I wasn't well, miss, I were poorly.' This was Polly Pearson's class. And, 'You're lying, you were seen in the cattle market.' 'Not me, miss.' You used to put your hands out, you knew what you were gonna get, three on each hand. But if you spit on 'em and put 'em under your arm, it used to gradually shift the pain off and I used to keep saying, 'Never mind, I got a bob for going. It was worth it'.

Andy Waudby remembers the cattle. He played in Walmgate with,

Nobby Briggs, Ronnie Cammidge who lived in Willow Street and Teddy Ottaway. We used to cut through to the cattle market. And we had what they called cow wallopers, and some of the chaps were lodging in Walmgate, and you could always see 'em with their sticks. One day they were bringing these bullocks to the station and they got away, come through the arches, and charging down

Walmgate. Everybody scattered, talk about a bull in a china shop, and we finished up through the gates of St Margaret's churchyard!

Albert Howard was able to earn something at the cattle market,

Used to go out at five o'clock on a morning and help 'em bring them in. Down Hull Road, used to let them take their time. All t'motor cars used to wait. If they started to come, it'd frighten 'em to death, start a stampede. Then take 'em back into t'cattle market, get 'em sorted out in pens and start curry-combing down and getting them ready for sale.

Everybody knew their own cattle. They were numbered in their ears. I walked 'em to t'field up at Osbaldwick. That's when I used to earn my money, and then I started to smoke. When I was eight! In them days they were cheap, five for tuppence. And then I used to run some pigs down to William Wright's, take 'em down Foss Islands.

Mr Stan Leaf, landlord of The Phoenix, recounts an amusing incident,

On one occasion, I happened to be standing outside Fishergate bar and looking on the bar walls and I saw this cow coming along. It had come up the steps near Walmgate Bar and it couldn't get down 'cos it's boarded in at the end. I had to ring the council and they sent someone with a key to open the gate there. The cow eventually jumped down onto the moat and let itself come through the gate, and through the bar and back to its pen. Anyone meeting it face to face, I don't know what they'd have done. It was a big drop down. I often wish I'd had a camera.

Dick Calpin recalls how his father-in-law, John Henry (Spud) Taylor, was a cattle drover. He suffered an accident, yet the family still managed to see the funny side of the situation,

He was kicked in the leg whilst working at the cattle pens, and had to have his leg amputated because gangrene set in. When Fanny [his wife] went to collect him from hospital, she discovered that she had cut the wrong leg out of his trousers!

The cattle market encouraged other businesses. Bushell's, the agricultural engineers, opened on the corner of Kent Street, and sold a variety of machinery for farmers. Kay and Backhouse, the agricultural implement makers, had their office on Foss Bridge and works in Walmgate.

Harry Lovick remembers Bushells,

Mr Bushell won a car in a national raffle about 1933 for half a crown. Now somebody knew Mr Bushell wanted to sell this car and my father bought it off him. It was an old Morris. Mawsons at the bottom end, they had a car, but I can't think of anybody else in Walmgate who had a car.

Bushells in cattle market 1940s

Strangeways hay and straw business in George Street supplied the cattle dealers. Mrs Elsie Precious grew up there,

I was born at 4 George Street right opposite the warehouse we had. Me Grandma Strangeway from Osbaldwick built the yard in George Street. I used to work on the cattle market at nights when I grew up, the hay men were working all night when the cattle were coming in. In those days they had to be fed when they got off the train and walked across to the pens. I used to help with the hay on Thursday, and put the straw or the hay down in the pens. The drovers fetched the hay on a little wheelbarrow from George Street when me mother was poorly. She was a worker was me mother. She worked all afternoon in the warehouse and it was the last bit of thing she did, weighed some hay up for Thursday morning. And she was dead. Certain of the family used to help out. We were all together.

An Array of Shops

Although there was industry in Walmgate, it is chiefly remembered for its vast array of shops, many of which enticed people from far and wide, with delicious foods.

Crow family
Standing, left to right: Fred Crow, Rev Duke, Hutchinson, Albert Crow
Middle row, left to right: Winnie Crow (marr. Rev Duke), Wm Wright,
Lucy Crow (marr. Hutchinson), Joe Crow
Front row, left to right: Walter Crow, Lizzie Crow (marr. Wm Wright),
name unknown (1st wife of Joe Crow)

Crows' butchers was located just within the Bar and anyone associated with Walmgate will not fail to mention the now-famous 'penny duck' which served as a nourishing meal for the local population. Anthony Gray is the nephew of the Crow sisters, whose ancestors came to York and founded the firm,

They came in 1860. In the 1800s my great great grandparents were the Fletchers who lived in Frieston on a farm, and they went into Market Rasen with the pork pies and meat pies and sold them from a basket. Albert, Selena, Joe and Walter Crow and the family came to live in Walmgate and spread out into business. Albert and Fred set up the pork butchers.

Albert Crow had three daughters, my mother Ada Winifred, Kathleen and Marjorie. My father married Ada Winifred, left Durham University where he was being educated and joined the business.

Crow's through Walmgate Bar

Mr Gray's grandparents lived in the Groves,

The pony and trap used to leave Walmgate with the sausages and the meat for their dinner and used to go all the way round the bar walls and take the food for me grandparent's meal. So they thought, 'While it's going there, we might as well have a shop here', so they opened the Townend Street shop.

Soon, other branches were opened, including ones in Acomb, Dringhouses, Haxby Road and elsewhere in the city. Anthony Gray came into the business himself,

Every week I used to buy 50 pigs, 10 bullocks, 40 sheep, to go to the eight shops, and the sows which made up for the pork pies and the sausages. Every week. We used to supply with two vans. William Wright delivered Crows pork pies on a bicycle from Walmgate shop and he married Elizabeth Crow. And they set up in Goodramgate.

Unfortunately increasing overheads and heavy traffic began to affect trade, as did the birth of the supermarket. But Mr Gray still has the recipes for some of his family's most popular dishes,

The cured hams. When you cook a joint at home, put it in a roasting bag, with brown sugar and honey and it goes right through it. And then roast it off with a bit of brown sugar or honey on top. That took the sting off it.

The penny ducks was the method of using all that was left. You used to sell your chops and your sausages and everything, but at the end of the day your penny ducks were squares, they were made in trays. Everything used to go in, used to boil all your bones. It was good meat, you just put gelatine with it and a colouring and you got super brawn. But everything that was left over was perfectly OK, was mashed up and then you added rusk to it, and onions, and sometimes fat, but usually it had enough fat of its own. Then you put 'em into trays, so it was a mixture of breadcrumbs, onions and everything that was left over. It was put through the mincer, and then put into trays and baked. And it was popular 'cos it was tasty, and it was cheap.

Crow's Butchers 1950s

Miss Rita Graham worked in the office at Crows from 1951 to 1957, earning one guinea a week. She remembers that Miss Kathleen and Miss Marjorie Crow owned a silver Bentley, which was sometimes driven by a companion. The factory and bakehouse were at the back of the shop and access was along a passage between Crows and Hutchinson the grocers. The shop often donated pies, sausages and meat to the Poor Clare's Convent in Lawrence Street. The nuns called regularly and there was always a package out for them.

When meat arrived from the cattle market, it was carried on the backs of the men, not an easy manoeuvre for the men to carry half a carcase on their backs. One day one of the men went through the passageway and then out into the open and he had to pass the office. I used to leave my bike outside the window. It must have been frosty and he slipped and dropped the whole carcass on my bike. The firm had it mended and by lunchtime it was there with a new wheel!

She also recalls how the takings were collected from the branches after closing time in a Gladstone bag and cashed up ready to be banked the following morning. The wages, worked out from a Kalamazoo system, were brought from the bank by van or even bicycle. There was no Securicor then, yet no trouble ensued.

She remembers the firm was generous to its employees, with regular staff outings to the coast, and dinners on special occasions. In 1960 the firm celebrated its centenary with a dinner at Betty's Restaurant. Each guest received either an embroidered handkerchief or a pen. The company also remembered birthdays,

For my 21st I was given five pounds. I spent 17/6 of it on a Mrs Beeton's Everyday Cookery Book and I still have that today thirty nine years later.

Walmgate c1940

Cambage's

Betty Thompson's family ran a greengrocer's shop at 134 Walmgate, called Cambage's,

My mother at 7 years old used to have to deliver fruit and veg to rich people, they used a large pram. She and her brother Harry would walk miles, right up Hull Road, and the people used to give them a piece of cake for the delivery.

Her father played the piano and the organ and her brothers played the trumpet for dances in York, they were a musical family. Most of the food they lived on in those days was bone broth, boiled tomatoes, big apple pies, custard, milk, boiled

potatoes, parsnips, carrots, swedes, in white sauce. It was all perfectly cooked. And they didn't have any sweets, they used to have to eat apples and little raspberries and gooseberries, being in the fruit shop. They had barrels outside with apples in. In those days they'd polish the apples and have them on display with little ribbons on. There was just me grandad in t'shop with a brown overall but I think all the kids were in the back somewhere.

They left there in 1935 because the big shops started taking over and there was no trade left. I remember they were selling matches in the street and my father allus used to buy some, for all you could buy them in the shops, helping them out a bit.

Rubye Readhead recalls,

A little corner shop sold a lot of sweets and odd bits of groceries. We used to buy sweets there, 'cos when you're a child you don't bother about hygiene. But she always looked as though she never had a wash, either herself or her clothes. She used to come into our house and was always borrowing things. I remember one day my father had come in from work, he'd had his meal and my mother was giving him some cake and a cup of tea. This lady lady came in and said, 'Oh I make lovely cakes, oh yes, I mix 'em with my hands'. And we all looked horrified, me father nearly dropped his tea, 'cos her hands were black. And after that, it became a family joke. If anyone came, we used to say, 'Did you mix them with your hands?'

The Bakers

Violet Quigley remembers,

Every Saturday morning, not only me mam but all t'women round about used to bake a stone of white bread and a stone of currant bread. And we used to have to take 'em down to Rowleys, one under each arm and one in front, three we'd take. And they used to bake 'em for ha'penny a loaf, and they had a little ticket on with your name. And when you went back for 'em about four o'clock, you were looking all over among t'bread for yours. Then through t'week she just used to bake bread-cakes in t'oven.

Ronald Jeffrey worked at Beaumonts at number 74, now Jenny's Kitchen,

I am a pacifist and during the Second World War, I was a baker's roundsman. I was working for a shop in Acomb and they sacked me because I was a conchie but Beaumonts, he was a real Old Testament character with a lot of hair and his son was a Quaker so he took me on there. I was absolutely convinced not to touch anything to do with the war, nothing at all. I worked at Beaumonts before the war and during the war, before I went to prison, and when I came out of prison I went in the same job.

Another lady explained that Beaumonts had a contract with the workhouse for food for tramps. The governor gave them a sixpenny slip, with which they could purchase a breadcake of brawn and mustard, and a small packet of Brooke Bond tea. The slips were then returned to the workhouse in exchange for cash.

Stan Cowen also called there,

On a Saturday night when I was a weekending lad, finishing at 9 o'clock, it used to be very very much alive in Walmgate. And most shops would be open. Beaumonts the bakers, the one thing I used to love getting from there was their vanilla slices.

And there was this fishmongers, Waudbys. It was all laid out on a slab, and they'd have running water coming down from the top of the slab to the bottom. Not only did they sell fish but hung around the side of the doors there'd be every sort of game that there was. I remember the proprietor, Wilf Waudby, and he had two golden retriever dogs.

Mrs Olive Waudby is the widow of Wilf Waudby. She worked for Fotheringham's plumbers at 63, at the top of George Street, (now a beauty salon) next door to the fishmonger's,

The Army and Navy store was next door before it was Fotheringham's. We were very friendly with the owners and we used to visit. These boys had a housekeeper and she was always having to keep them in order and we used to laugh about these boys next door, never thinking that later on I should marry one of them.

When we were in our teens, we used to go to dances. The Storeys [from the Army and Navy], when they bought the shop at the top of Fossgate, moved to East Mount Road. So we used their empty bedrooms, the staff and friends, on a Wednesday afternoon, we'd learn to dance.

Butchers

Rubye Readhead remembers a butcher named Cade's at 55 Walmgate, whose succulent beef was famous in the area, with customers coming from farther afield to buy it,

There was sawdust on the floor. Inside the door, which was always open, was a bulldog. It was like a door stop. I was terrified to go in there, but I learnt later it was a real softie. Another butcher across the road used to make soup in the thirties and sell it in jugs for poor people. It was damn good soup, with all the meat and stock from the bones.

The Dent family had been butchers in Walmgate since the mid-19th century. George Dent was one of the earliest, and died aged 59 in 1878, at his home in Osbaldwick Grange. The last person to have lived at the butcher's premises at 138 next door to the Angel, is Mrs Mary Dent,

I married Jack Dent at the outbreak of war, in 1939. Dent's were a big business, butchers and game dealers. They supplied Fulford barracks, the sergeants' mess and Strensall common. They'd always had Heslington shop which supplied Heslington Hall when Lord Deramore was there.

Sheila White remembers Dent's,

Mr Dent worked until nine o'clock on a Saturday night selling and on a Sunday morning he'd get up and go to church and take Brandy his dog for a walk, and then he would open the shop and he'd sell off all that was left. He used to have the shop cleared out then, and it would all be washed and swilled out and all the wood would be brushed down, and he would start again, go across to the cattle market on the morning and bid for his beast. Because they were all on the hoof in those days, people didn't have frozen stuff.

The butchers would also make chitterling sausages, by cooking the intestines of the pigs until they were tender.

Terry Kilmartin recalls,

I lived at 1 Huby's Passage and I stopped there while I was ten. It was an experience of a lifetime because there was four slaughterhouses and each Monday and Friday they used to kill and the bullocks and the pigs were squealing all night. Mr Dent's son was six foot six and he used to pick sheep up and put 'em on a rack, and stab 'em and clean 'em and skin 'em and everything. And he used to get the bullock's eyes and pop 'em and they used to squirt out at you. But he was very good to us, he used to give us money for collecting the eggs from the hens and cleaning 'em out.

Me dad had such a love of animals that we went to the Golden Barrel yard and we had 80 odd pigs down there during the war. You was allowed to kill one, but they used to kill two or three and swap it for sugar and everything else that was going. Me dad kept Hope Street going, the old people, with offal and that, and in fact you never realised how many friends you had when they got to know you'd killed a pig.

Fish Shops

The owner of Ellerkers also bought the shop on the corner of Walmgate and Merchantgate and his grand-daughter Pat Daker recalls,

He made it into a fish and chip shop. And Auntie Florrie used to run it. The fish came in whole and she had to gut it and clean all the potatoes and chip them. I'd go in and she always had her head in a pan. I used to go 'boo' and she'd say, 'You'll have me in this pan one of these days'. When the river came up, it flooded, and that was the end. No fish and chips until it went down. There was two shops in Walmgate, Auntie Florrie on the corner and Alice Leckenby halfway up. Alice couldn't go to school until she'd seen to t'fish.

Alice Leckenby's family ran the fish shop near the bar, which had once been St Peter's Vaults public house. When Alice married, it became Hall's.

School Street corner shop

Sheila White remembers,

In Hall's fish shop, you could go three mornings a week, Monday, Thursday and Friday and they used to hold wet fish at the side entrance. And then they would fry and be open for the farmers on Monday and Thursday, and Friday lunchtime they opened for everyone. In those days they did a big trade, with it being a catholic community, they didn't eat meat on a Friday. They had three waitresses behind the counter serving and two men frying and it never differed. Everything was beautiful, you could have anyone to dinner and serve that up to them.

Terry Kilmartin remembers,

Down Ancroft Street, there's a bloke called Brown and he used to push an ice-cream cart. Some o't kids would give him a push and get a biscuit off him. And two or three times they'd leave him halfway up and he could hardly move,

and they'd say, 'If you aren't gonna give me ice-cream, I aren't gonna push you any more'.

Olive Waudby recalls,

There was a little shop nearly opposite to us in George Street, and it was a spinster that had it, Nelly Clapham. She was like something out of a book. She looked as if she'd seen a ghost, her hair used to stick out and we'd be able to buy a bar of chocolate for half a penny. During the war, I earned many a bright penny. There was a place called Chapel Row, and 'There's a ha'penny for you if you come and tell me when there's any treacle at the stores'. I used to get the jam jars and go to the Co-operative Stores in George Street for one lot of treacle for every ration book. Then collect the ration books and collect the penny.

Sheila White recalls,

Next to the Bar was Hutchinsons, a choice provisions shop. He used to have big gammons hung up in the window, beautiful ham and beautiful cheeses. And good bacon. If you went to Mr Hutchinson, it was all special, and when he served he always had his hat on. He used to have two butter paddles, like cricket bats, and he'd pat the butter and cut you a piece off, two ounces, four ounces, six ounces, whatever you wished. And he would cut the cheeses. You could have a two ounce

Hutchinson's Shop near the Bar

piece or whatever or a little bit of each. Now you've got to have what's in package and the weight they put on it.

Opposite St Denys's church was Nellis's. That building has been boarded up for 20 years, never sold. You could go in there and get anything from a small screw to an electric light socket, and he used to sell radiators, stoves, cookers, you name it.

Lillian Prior liked,

One particular shop that belonged to two maiden ladies, Misses Hawksbys. A funny little shop, you went down some steps into it and it didn't have a door. It had a gate and the bell rang, and they sold the most gorgeous cooked ham which they made themselves.

Although Walmgate had an excellent range of shops, the tradesmen selling their wares from a horse and cart were a feature until the Second World War, as Mrs Mary Jeffrey explains,

A chap used to come all the way from Overton selling milk, and then a chap called Jimmy Gilligan would come with bananas, eight for sixpence, and another day he would come with herrings.

Rubye Readhead remembers,

A rag and bone man used to come round. You got a goldfish if you took so many rags to him, with a jam jar, and the poor thing only lived about two days. Then there was a man used to come round every Sunday about two o'clock with a handcart selling ice-cream. You could take a drinking tumbler and you would get that full of ice-cream with two wafers for tuppence. And that was the treat of the week. Our milkman used to come from Heslington. He had a pony and trap, all the wood was a beautiful golden varnish and the milk was in churns. He never seemed to have to tell the horse when to stop, it knew which house he had to stop at. You took your jug out and he had a measure which hooked onto the side of the milk churn and he'd measure out what you wanted.

Mary Booker recalls,

Mr Swann the milkman had like a trap, just to step on and a little door to open and three great big milk churns. One day he never put the top on the milk churn, and a woman opened the door and her dog run out and it was yapping and barking and horses rearing. All t'milk was running out, and there was all dogs coming out and la-la-la [lapping it up]. And t'man there had a monkey on a great big chain, and it was trying to get to the milk on the floor and he was battling to get it back in this yard. And all t'dogs and cats was licking the milk.

The area was not just famous for its range of foodstuffs, but sold almost everything else you could think of!

Lovick's

Harry Lovick and his parents ran a draper's shop for many years. His mother started the business in 1915 when his father was still on war work,
My mother was a dressmaker by trade, apprenticed to a lady on Huntington Road. In those days before the First War, people who were middle-class had all their clothes made.

When my father was out of his apprenticeship, which I would assume would be five years, he and grandfather went into partnership in Walmgate, where they were joiners and undertakers. It didn't work so grandfather went his own way and my father started working for himself as a self-employed joiner and undertaker in about 1908. I've heard him say that a coffin before the First War cost about £8.

Insurance in those days would be no more than mebbe a penny or tuppence a week, and people had some pride so they weren't buried on the parish. They would buy a little bit of insurance so they had £8. I've heard me father say, soon as they got the funeral over, they used to go straight back to the house and get the money because otherwise once they got the tears out of their eyes, they didn't want to pay.

Harry Lovick Snr. and Jnr.

But soon, Mr Lovick senior opened the drapery business at 130 Walmgate, next to the Bay Horse Inn,

In the '30s there were six drapers in Walmgate, and I suppose at the beginning, my parents found it pretty tough going. But my father had a real flair for buying. I can remember when I was a boy, I started going with him to Leeds. I left school in 1937 and then I went with him buying.

We sold a lot of baby clothes, that was probably our best line - napkins, baby gowns, wrapper vests. When I was a little boy, ladies in Walmgate never wore overcoats, all they wore was a black shawl which they'd put over their heads and

round their shoulders. We sold our cheapest men's cap for one shilling, five pence in new money and our most expensive cap was half a crown.

We used to say we could clothe a lady from getting out of the bath to walking down the street for one pound. We used to sell shoes made in Czechoslovakia, 25 pence a pair, ladies' stockings, silk or cotton, would be 5 pence a pair. A pair of corsets would be 15 pence, a set of underwear 15 pence, a blouse no more than 20 pence. We used to sell a pair of men's shoes, all leather, for about fifty pence in modern money, which today sounds absolutely fantastic. They were probably imported. Of course, Walmgate in my boyhood was nothing but little businesses. There would be I should think, ten butchers, half a dozen grocers, three or four greengrocers, three or four sweet and tobacco shops.

We opened on a Sunday morning for two hours until about 1936 when the law changed. Shop hours in those days were very long, from eight in a morning until eight at night, and nine on a Saturday. Christmas Eve it would be ten thirty or eleven, and still people would be knocking.

Things started to improve up to the start of the war. Business was really good. People were working, had money to spend. They could buy meat, fish, eggs, butter - things that the poor people of the '30s simply couldn't afford. The dreadful irony of the war years, a lot of people ate better then than they had before.

In 1941, the government brought in clothes rationing, and that went on until about 1949. By then people's wardrobes were down, they wanted to replenish them and business through the '50s was very very good. Prices clearly were much cheaper than they are today. There was virtually no inflation. But then supermarkets started up in the '60s and the little man started to hit some very hard times.

Andy Waudby remembers,

Me granny took me to this draper's shop, I think it was Lovicks. Up to then I'd always had short trousers, oh I did look a charlie in 'em, they come come below your knees. And she bought me these grey flannel trousers and a white shirt so

74

we went home and it was the day I left school. I put these trousers on and immediately I felt like a man, and she says, 'You're going out into the world now and you'll find it's a very hard place' and by God it was.

Mike Race recalls another draper's shop near the bar, which was probably Smith's at 170 Walmgate,

They also sold children's toys. I can remember seeing just after the war, this wondrous display of toys in the window and underneath it said, 'Join our Christmas club'. So I decided to have these toys, and it said sixpence a week. I thought, 'We can afford that'. I must have been about eight or nine, so I went in and joined this Christmas club. I went home and told me mother and she went whizzing round to the shop and gave the woman a piece of her mind for letting small boys join the Christmas club without their parents being with them. So I never got the toys and I never joined the Christmas club.

There was one shop which me mother used to point out to me, just after the war when rationing was still on. He was supposed to be a centre for the black market and confectionery. This was a very small shop and I remember me mother watching two policemen. Plain-clothes policemen in those days might as well have worn uniforms 'cos they were so easily identified. They all wore trilbies and trench-coats. A CID man, you could see him a hundred yards away. I remember watching these two policemen go in and me mother saying, 'There they go, to get their bit from the black market'.

Ellerker's

Betty Pollard and her sister Pat Daker are the grand-daughters of Ralph Ellerker, another well-known business in Walmgate. It began initially in Church Street, then moved to 62 Walmgate, before establishing the shop at 25, a property owned by the Ecclesiastical Commissioners, which sold,

Saddles and ropes and halters. Everything for horses, brasses, the lot. And then he made his own ropes and his own tarpaulins and stack nets, anything agricultural really, apart from machinery.

75

Thomas Driver, son-in-law of Ralph Ellerker
at Ellerker's

Mr Ellerker had workshops at the rear of the premises, and took in apprentices. One of his grand-daughters still has a small chair with a low back where he would sit to splice his ropes with a cow horn. Ralph Ellerker had a pony and trap and conducted a great deal of his business in the cattle market,

He would have the baskets absolutely chock-a-block. They're on wheels and that would be full of goods for sale. He was an auctioneer as well, used to auction off the ropes, saddles and horse collars. My father was a sidesman at St Denys's Church in Mr Leng's day. Grandfather used to make the ropes for the bells. And he always had a stock of candles and gave them to the church when they wanted candles. And the last time the church was carpeted, he carpeted it out with that thick sisal matting 'cos it's stone floor down the sides.

They used to say there was more money made in Walmgate than the whole of York put together.

Ellerker's

But the business was affected when war came,

In the Second World War, the horses had almost disappeared. The tractor had taken over and the backbone of the business had gone.

Father kept it going for a number of years, used to make his ropes, coalbags and tarpaulins, and wagon ropes.

Ralph Ellerker was also commissioned to make hangman's nooses and,

The safety net for the Zambezi river. For the government. And he used to supply, through a London rubber company, the police with waterproofs. Grandfather's ropery, when he made the long ropes, was from Walmgate Bar to George Street Bar, and he used to stand on the Bar Walls and watch the ropes being made. It was very interesting to watch the saddles being made and the horse collars being repaired. These big horse collars, all stuffed with straw. And checked material put over that.

Andy Waudby visited Ellerkers,

With my cousins and we used to get a rope or a cord and it was tarbine and they'd put it round the dog's neck and that was supposed to keep distemper away. The younger the dog, the better, and this turbine, it smelt beautiful. It was put round all the whippets, if it worked I don't know.

The Bookmakers

Another way to make a bit of cash was to be a bookie's runner. Several people in the area did this, including Joyce Burnett's mother,

She took bets and I used to take them up for her to the bookie's. You get so much in the pound. My dad used to take it to work, do it and lock it up. They used to go in t'bag and it was timed so people couldn't go into it while after t'first race.

Rubye Readhead recalls,

In George Street was a lady called Mrs Bardy, she had a longish back yard with a strip of garden. And she had knocked a hole in the brickwork and ran a little betting shop from there. And you could have threepence each way or sixpence to win or whatever. About every month she'd get whipped into the police station and fined five shillings, because it was against the law in those days. But she still carried on. She had a huge family and she was a widow.

Brian Douglass remembers,

I used to go to me grandmother's betting shop most lunchtimes. The front of the shop had obviously been a draper's, by the size of the shelves and the counters and it was a cover for the betting at the back but over the years she came to an agreement with the police where they raided her every month, took her away and she paid a fine and they brought her back. You went through the shop, the staircase went up to your left and she was laid out on a chaise-longue near the big table with the money and the betting slips and I just sat in the little kitchen. If it was a good day I got a fourpence-ha'penny meat and potato pie, if it was a bad day I got a penny savoury duck from Crows'.

There was a shop right opposite the Malt Shovel, and he used to do a deal with comics. You'd take one in and he'd buy it off you for a ha'penny and then sell it for a penny. Or else you could take two comics and swap it for one. And the shop on the corner was the chip shop and they used to do us ha'penny bags of chips as a special. Eventually they had to put them up to a penny and there was nearly a riot. When sweets became scarce during the war, one shop right up near the bar had a window full of liquorice root. We ate what we could for so long but then it started to have an affect on your bowels. I can never touch it now.

Many people mention Matty Myers, the newsagent and bookie at 120 Walmgate. He opened in business in 1912, and also had premises in Castlegate from 1920. Although an invalid all his life, he ran a successful business until his death in May 1941. Alf Ottaway recalls Matty as a generous man,

Every Tuesday he went to George Bradley's hairdressers. It was usually full on that day, they knew Matty would pay for them.

Harry Lovick recalls that,

Billy Burke would say that his father used to go to Matty Myers's and they'd play cards all night and he had beer and whisky and gin and anything you wanted. Presumably that was the man's bit of enjoyment out of life.

Chemists

Mrs Jeffrey explains how the chemist's shop at 102 Walmgate, was more like a doctor's surgery,

If you went to Mrs Falconer, she'd give you a bottle of medicine. Funnily enough when we left the town and went to Osbaldwick, who did we find but Mrs Falconer, she'd a big house there. And she used to walk to York and back every day. And always dressed like a nurse with white sleeves with elastic round, above the elbows.

Mrs Booker also knew the lady,

She was in the chemist, great big place and they had loads of bottles, patterned red and green all round, and loads of little drawers. Mrs Falconer was real tall and slim and had lovely hair up in a bun and wore all blue and a white apron, just like a nurse. Everybody used to go to her to see what was matter.

Between 1871 and 1969, the shop had undergone several name changes, being variously occupied by Leak, Lockwood, Snowdon, Enderby, Robinson, Myers, Campbell and Falconer, Falconer and Mitchell, and Dales.

When Mr Leak was in charge in 1871, he advertised his own special preparations, such as Leak's Cough Mixture, Leak's Tic Doloreux Mixture, Leak's aperient pills and Leak's stomach pills, all for a shilling each.

There was another chemist and druggist at 154 Walmgate, Thomas Batty. Although he died in 1901, the shop continued as a chemist right until the 1940s. Harry Lovick's mother would go there for a home-made remedy,

She used to keep goose grease from Christmas and with two pennyworth of camphorated oil from Batty's, it was used to rub chests.

Batty's would prescribe various concoctions, such as laudanum and oil for earache, oil of violets and almonds for sore throats, and liquorice powder and turkey rhubarb for lazy bowels.

As well as selling 'genuine drugs and chemicals', he also supplied oils and paints, tea, coffee, tobacco, cigars, spices, perfumes, and fancy soaps. Reg Lambert remembers that Thomas Batty was a registrar, as well as a chemist.

Shopkeepers were often not confined to one product, but had many goods on offer. At number 80 Walmgate, T. Cooper operated as a chemist in the 1870s, but also recommended a medicine chest for disorders in horses, cattle, calves, sheep and lambs, for a mere 21 shillings. He advocated that 'every farmer ought to have one'.

Walmgate shops c1907

The Pawnbroker

Addie Haythorne's pawnbroker's at 121 Walmgate was always busy, especially on a Monday morning when locals took their Sunday best in to be pawned until the following Friday. The shop also ran savings clubs. Olive Hardy remembers the 'Christmas didlum', where you paid 1/1d a week all year and got a lump sum back at Christmas to buy your presents. Dolly Corrigan's mother would lend poor people her jewellery to pawn, as they had nothing else. She remembers buying goods 'on the chucky', which meant paying weekly.

Walmgate Bar

For some people, going to the pawnbroker's was a way of life, for some people more than others, as Violet Quigley explains,

There was a couple living in Smith's Buildings, and they used to go on the beer, and get really drunk, and pawn everything in the house. They finished up without anything and he used to draw all pictures on t'wall of sofas and furniture, all round. And when they'd finished this spell of drinking, they'd go tee-total and sit day and night pegging long pricked hearthrugs. Then sell them and get everything out of pawn.

Mary Booker's mother,

was real soft-hearted. People used to go to her and say, 'Our Tom, he ha'nt got a bit bite nor sup, can you lend us two bob?'. Me mam got known, she was Lady Bountiful for everybody round there. She had a lot of jewellery and lovely clothes and she used to say, 'I can't help you with money' but she'd lend her earrings and jewellery. Haythorne's pawnshop was in Walmgate and they used to take them there and they'd get mebbe whatever, and me mam was proper soft.

Shoe Repairers

Peter Stanhope has traced the history of his family back to the days of his great grandfather's brother, John Lakin Gibson, who had a boot and shoeshop at 69 Walmgate. The shop is now Faunus Florists, and the present owner is constructing a Victorian garden at the rear.

Gibson was a churchwarden at St Margaret's church, and his father Mark had been a coach trimmer for a firm of livery, lace, tassel and web weavers.

Peter recalls visiting the shop when he was a boy,

I went in to see Aunt Bessie who was very old. She lived behind the shop and I can always remember, she was quite grumpy but she had this very decorative harmonium in the parlour. As a small child I could sit up at it and pedal like mad and press the keys and get some noises out of it. It was a colour that I now know to be yew, had a yellowish look about it, very heavily fretted, very decorative, so they must have had money. Because your average family didn't have a harmonium.

Going into the shop which was now defunct, it was quite ghostly because there were shelves and shelves that were empty, the odd box of shoes remaining. And the deep blue blinds that you used to pull down with cords, were down at the front of the shop.

The proximity of the cattle market gave rise to other trades, and leather by-products in the area. There were saddlers, harness-makers and cordwainers, as Peter Stanhope, a member of the Company of Cordwainers of the city of York, explains,

The meat was for consumption, the entrails were taken in another direction, and the hides were tanned and curried and then converted into shoes, not yet boots, but shoes by the cordwainers who centred on St Denys's church. In 1600 the guild of cordwainers was fifty strong. By 1831, the census reports 447 boot and shoe makers in the city of York. In 1977 the company of cordwainers was reformed in the city.

Stubbs

Before Stubbs took over their present shop, Foss Bridge House, (built in 1878), it was the location of William Whitehead, the draper, who died in 1884. The black iron gate beside the front door still has the initials WW in the railings. Francis Richard Stubbs began his trade in Lady Peckett's Yard and he died in March 1915 at the age of 57.

Three Cups, now part of Stubbs

Today, Mr Bill Stubbs, the third generation, also owns the house next door, a listed building which is used for additional storage space. It was built in 1830 and became a public house, the Three Cups, in approximately 1850. (The Red Lion, now in Merchantgate, was also called the Three Cups until 1805). The pub closed in 1907. Maureen Aspinall recalls that an old lady lived there in the Second World War, and the present carpark was an attractive garden,

We used to go down there to get in that back garden. Where the cars are, it was all trees then and Tarzan was on the go. We used to wait till she'd gone in t'house 'cos she used to sit on a chair at the door. Then we'd get on our hands and knees and go by this window so she didn't see us. We used to go and play Tarzan in t'trees, I had bruises all over, me mother used to say, 'You should have been a lad'. We'd swing from tree to tree till she found us, then she'd throw us out, go and tell me mother and I'd be in trouble.

There is a passage in this house which leads down to the river. The old range is still in situ, with the inscription from Dove's ironmongers (originally the apprentice of Thomlinson-Walker).

Stubbs the Ironmongers 1996

Foss Bridge House is a rather grand building, with five storeys and a total of 37 rooms! Most of the rooms are used as storage for the vast array of tools and equipment for which the shop is renowned. The slogan of the shop is 'Better buy on the bridge', and every possible item of ironmongery is available there.

Mr Bill Stubbs and staff - Susie Stubbs, Tracey Beck
and Barry Newton at Stubbs 1996

The top floor, or attic, has labels on each of the doors, for the Billiard Room, Classroom, Recreation Room, Museum and Scouts Patrol Room, obviously stemming from the days when Scouts used the rooms, as did the Liberal Club. The front room has an excellent view of the Minster, and contains the old billiard table, paraffin heater, and original Victorian flock wallpaper and fireplaces. Another room on this floor also has the old winch, with a lift used to move materials.

Some time ago, a member of York Civic Trust wrote to the Evening Press describing the shop as having dirty, grimy windows. In response, Mr Stubbs suspended an effigy from one of his windows, wearing an apron and clutching a mop!

There is a separate passage beside the front door, leading up a back staircase, which was used as an entrance for the billiard hall. Sheila White's

Dad's aunt had Parker's Hotel. Stubbs's, that was hers. And they had a snooker room upstairs and a dance-hall, when I was a child.

The 1925 street directory mentions the Premier Dance Academy on Foss Bridge, which taught 'all classes of dancing', and specialised in carnivals and gala nights. It claimed to be the 'most commodious rooms in the city'.

Barges

At one time, barges were a familiar sight on the two rivers of the city. Now the only working barges are those run by Graham Acaster of Acaster Transport. Graham's son is the fifth generation of the Acaster family to work the river.

Graham Acaster (right) and son (left) with Dave Jarvis, Warehouse Manager at the Yorkshire Evening Press, on a barge at Wormald's Cut, 1996

They operate two tugs, Little Shifta and Little Shova, which push the four lighters (adapted to be pans, which are about twenty five years old) along the Foss from Goole to Wormald's Cut, behind the Yorkshire Evening Press, delivering paper which comes originally from Scandinavia.

River Star on the Foss 1996

The lighters are named Poem 24, Kirkby, River Star and Twite and they have recently acquired a barge, with motorised engine, called the Libra. At one time the editor could name his price, but since Eastern Europe came into the free market, the price of paper has rocketed, hence the importing. Two lighters together contain 240 tons of paper. 100 tons of paper is the equivalent of five articulated lorryloads, and will last for three days. This includes not just the Press, but also the Gazette and Herald, the Star and the Northern Echo. Between 12,500 and 15,000 tons a year are brought to the printers. Before the Press moved to Walmgate from Coney Street, the wharf was used for grain and animal feed, fish meal and maize coming from Hull. Sand was delivered to Walkers, and cocoa beans were transported to Rowntrees warehouse (once Leethams

Mill). The Foss was a busy place. When the Press moved to its new premises in 1988, they had to make sure that this part of the river was navigable and that the boats could get through the smallest lock. Kirkby is 97 foot long and the nearest lock is 98 foot, so it will only just fit.

Ray D had a business down Walmgate in the 1960s,

Removals and haulage and barges. I run barges, for what was a firm at the end of Poad's Yard, we used to bring grain back from Hull for them. And on the right hand side I kept me lorries. It was a pound a ton from York to Hull, you went into t'King George dock. I had two barges there, Steadfast and Venture, they carried hundred ton apiece. I used to skipper one meself. I had Steadfast and me other skipper was Ted Rook from Goole. The boatman's right of way ran from Beaumont's old bakery, directly through what is now the carpark of the Yorkshire Evening Press and down to where you picked up your cockboat to go to your main boat. The cockboat or cocky boat is the safety boat that you carry in case your barge gets into trouble.

Printing presses at the Yorkshire Evening Press 1996

The foundation stone of the Yorkshire Evening Press was laid on 17th November 1988 by the Chairman of Westminster Press, the Duke of Atholl. A time capsule was buried underneath the building by the Lord Mayor, which contained many objects relating to the 20th century and Walmgate. These included the book, 'And Proud of it Too', a York Oral History tape of local accents, a calculator, menu from Betty's, Argos catalogue, and a blue smartie.

Watchmakers

Mr Hick, the watchmaker and jeweller, was based at 66 Walmgate at the end of the 19th century. He sold gold watches for £5, and fashionable silver watches for 25s, with timepieces a mere 5s 6d. His clocks, at £1. 2s. 6d, were guaranteed to strike for eight days.

A rather sad tale surrounds the 62 year old clock maker of 106 Walmgate, Frederick (Clocky) Bracewell. Mrs Booker recalls him,

He used to sell pot ornaments, little boys and girls, and he'd fill 'em so t'little boys used to wee. He used to make us all laugh when we were kids. I used to take his laundry and I went across this day and he's sat on a big chair, and he's got a thing in his mouth and he's blue. I run across to Mr Robinson and said, 'Come and see him quick', so he went across and he said, 'Silly bugger, he backed a horse yesterday, Fleet Jack. He's won loads of money and it's gone to his head', and he got police.

Alf Ottaway remembers that Mr Bracewell had backed a winner at 100 to 1 and the shock killed him. The cemetery report of October 1924 gave the cause of death as heart failure.

Today there is still a clockmaker in the street, carrying on one of the ancient traditions. Doran's has been at 104 Walmgate since 1985. The shop was originally 102, Falconer's chemist, and next to Bracewell's. The owner personally restored the building when he moved in. He makes a few clocks but mostly repairs them. The oldest one he has repaired was a single-handed thirty hour long case clock with a brass dial, from 1730. At that time clocks only had one hand to tell the hours, there was no standard time throughout the country until the advent of railways made timetables necessary.

Mr M Doran, Clockmaker, 1996

Mr Doran's workshop is at the back of the shop, where he sits surrounded by clocks of all shapes and sizes. He uses a clockmaker's loupe over his left eye (most clockmakers use their right eye) and he has different loupes in different strengths, including one with ten times magnification for checking the balance springs on watches.

Mr Doran owns the public clock outside the shop, which he put in place as a service to the people of Walmgate.

There were other types of work going on in the area. Ray D remembers the onion sellers who came to the Five Lions,

I think they were from Normandy these lads, and they came every season to York, with their onions. They lived in the stables in the Five Lions yard which are now all demolished, lived and slept in there with the horses and paid the landlord a couple of bob a week. But what they did in there was to dress all their onions, twist them, put 'em into strings, hang them on the handlebars of the bike and go round York selling them.

He also remembers the Dollar Princess,

Directly opposite the Full Moon and to the right, down there was Cussins and Lights. William Holley and Pop Lawson had this open charabanc, this big canvas sheet came over the top, and it finished up by the Brewery. And they broke it up down there. Beautiful old thing. One of the first old charabancs.

Maureen Aspinall's parents worked on the fairground,

When the fairs come at Easter and Whitsuntide, me mother and father had stalls. Me Dad had a warehouse, the garage on the corner, and he used to make all these Mickey Mouses. Cut 'em out and paint 'em and sell 'em on the market with balloons. They were made of wood, a piece of wood in the middle, and a stick and they used to walk. Never seen them since those days. I used to stand on the market with them and me mother used to have a second hand stall.

My husband was down in Beans's yard and he sold logs. He used to have a big saw machine and I'd go down on afternoon or evening, playing down t'yard and he'd cut these logs up, put wire round and it was a bundle of sticks to make your fire. They had a horse and cart down there and he'd go out selling them. I was only thirteen but I had a crush on him, he was lovely.

Lillian Prior recalls,

A hat shop and when the Duke and Duchess came to York before they were married, the Duchess wore a blue velvet toque hat and my mother went to see them. She came home raving about this hat, nattered on about it and my father got so fed up of hearing her, he said, 'For goodness sake, Ethel, will you go and buy that hat, and then we'll hear the last of it'. So she did and she wore it until it practically fell off her head.

Rubye Readhead also remembers a rag shop,

Down the lane from George Street into Piccadilly, was Dixon's Lane, and at the top was a door. There was no windows, just like the black hole of Calcutta, and it was where Raggy Dixon sorted his rags. My brother hated school, he was always playing hookey. My father came home one mid-morning, he worked for the LNER and he'd been sent out to buy paint and he thought he'd call home for a cup of tea. He said, 'Do you know I've just seen a little lad sitting on Raggy Dixon's doorstep, helping him to sort the rags, and he's the image of our Peter'. And me mother said, 'It can't be him, he's been at school a good two hours'. Anyway it was Peter, he'd been there all morning.

If you went through George Street, there was the City Arms, and it was a stop for coaches from the West Riding going to the coast. And Peter decided he wouldn't go to school this particular summer morning, it was too nice. So he ambled through the bar and into the yard. There was a coach and it was empty 'cos all the men had gone in for their breakfast, and he climbed in and had a good look around. Before he could get out, the men started coming back, he didn't know what to do, so he crawled under the back seat. And he went all the way to Scarborough and had a wonderful time because he wandered up and down the beach and attached himself to families. So they'd feed him but when it came to teatime, they all dispersed to their various boarding-houses. My mother and father had reported him missing, and at eight o'clock at night, the policeman found him sitting on a pavement with his feet in the gutter. He didn't seem to be a bit bothered, so they put him in the police car and brought him home, and he just said, 'Oh, it's been marvellous. I've had a ride in a police car. I think I'm going to be a policeman when I grow up'. Me mother said, 'You'll be lucky!'

5

Little Ireland

Between 1846 and 1851, there were several potato famines in Ireland which devastated the country. Over a million of the population died of starvation and another million emigrated to Britain and the USA. Of the latter, many more died before reaching their destination, and the stories of how they were squeezed like animals into the holds of ships make horrific reading. Those who left their own land behind, imagining a better country, were doomed to disappointment, encountering another kind of misery. Dr Frances Finnegan in her academic study of the Irish in York, 'Poverty and Prejudice', and Sheelagh Kelly in her fictionalised accounts of the subject, have written in detail of the sufferings and anguish of the immigrants in Walmgate.

The Foss at end of Dennis Street

Irish families in yard in Dennis Street

There was a small Irish population in York before the famine, but afterwards the numbers increased enormously. Although there was as yet little in the way of industrial opportunity at that period, York was very close to a strong agricultural area, crying out for labour to work the land. Chicory, cattle, and other forms of agriculture attracted the Irish, and many of them actually came across the sea with the cattle. The docks at Foss Islands Road was a point where they would get their first glimpse of the city. Others arrived at the port of Liverpool and then set out to walk to York and other towns, some because they already had relatives here, and others because they had heard there was work available. The coming of the railways was another factor.

Walmgate, as one of the poorest areas of York, already had an Irish community, and this is where large numbers headed upon their arrival. Most of them were forced to live in overcrowded, insanitary conditions in the little courts and yards off the main street, close to slaughterhouses, breweries, mills and other manufacturers. The air must have been constantly black with pollution and the infant mortality rate was certainly above the average. In the 1860s there were allegedly 53 yards branching off Walmgate, and many of these were filled with hovels and tenements squeezed into the tiniest of spaces. Frances Finnegan cites Britannia Yard as an example, which had sixteen cottages in 1851, fifteen of which housed Irish families. The number of Irish totalled 171 in just that one yard! It was not until 1933 that it was demolished.

It has been well documented how it was the Quakers, and in particular Samuel Tuke and his son James who showed the most concern for the newcomers. The Tukes had visited various counties in Ireland to inspect the situation, and witness at first hand the effects of the famine.

By 1850 the outbreak of typhus, or Irish fever as it became known, which was particularly rampant in Walmgate, forced the authorities to open a temporary fever hospital, which was replaced by a permanent building in 1881. The Irish were, of course, as the newcomers, blamed for most of the problems and the crime, though Finnegan provides evidence that the Irish community actually committed less crimes than the host population. And when war broke out, one Irish family were amongst the first to volunteer to fight for their adopted country.

The local newspaper in 1914 featured an article about the Calpins, who lived at 38 Albert Street. The first members of the family had come from County Mayo in the south of Ireland, and when the First World War began, they became local celebrities, with ten Calpin brothers, the sons of Paddy and Sarah, enlisted in the British forces. The Lord Mayor, Henry Rhodes Brown, wrote, in a letter to the parents, 'It will be hard for anyone in the empire to equal your fine record of ten sons all serving their Country'. What was even more amazing was that all ten returned from the war, although John was gassed and died in hospital soon after, which left his wife Lizzie to bring up their seven children alone.

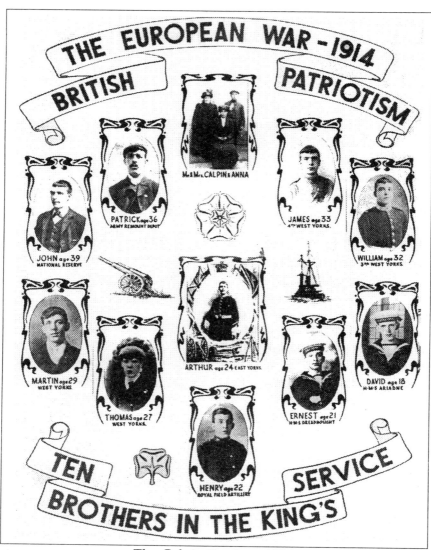

The Calpin Brothers 1914

Ernest's son, Owen Calpin, born in Long Close Lane, was one of eleven children. Owen's maternal side were the Loftus family, also from Mayo. Owen Loftus (Owen Calpin's namesake) had been a farmer in Ireland but was reduced to labouring when he settled in York. He married Bridget Durkin, one of a well-known Irish family. Martin Durkin, whose family arrived after the potato famine, was born in 1889, one of fourteen brothers and sisters. He died in 1993, at the age of 103 and claimed that the secret of his longevity was a daily bowl of porridge.

As a young boy, Owen liked nothing better than to sit in the house with his grandparents on long winter nights, and listen to the 'yarns'.

They lived in Hope Street, their back way was facing our passage. On dark nights it was lovely to listen to these old people, six or seven old Irishmen sitting round the fire. If they did say anything against the English, it used to go over my head, 'cos I was listening for the stories from Ireland.

His grandfather talked of having driven a stagecoach, or 'six-in-hand' from Ballinaire to Sligo, through wild open country, often chased by the nomads, 'who would cut your throat for a threepenny bit'. As the story progressed, a sudden shout of 'you great thundering liar' would come from the corner where his wife sat sucking her small clay pipe. She had heard the tales many times before!

A necessary accompaniment to the get-togethers would be the drinking of poteen, (whisky made from an illicit still, and traditionally very potent). It was certainly brewed in Walmgate.

Tommy [Owen's uncle] was the educated one. He was shot down in the artillery balloon over France. He had all kinds of recipes for this stuff, but I never got to taste it. The more they got, the more they spoke, and the more interesting, and the lies got bigger. It was entertaining, I loved it. Me granny used to drink porter, which is stout, a dark beer. I remember them filling a big jug up out of a barrel and then filling their glasses up on t'table.

Owen also recalls that the tales of Ireland and the 'old days' inevitably brought forth an emotional response, and the men would often cry,

They wa'nt in hysterics, you'd just see the tears coming down their eyes. Don't forget they was fresh over here. They'd left one devastated area to come into

another. Sometimes I wonder where they were worse off. The Irish immigrants in Walmgate especially was equivalent to the travelling people now and how they were resented by most of the population. Which they are.

It was a community, the Irish people. There was English families with 'em but they tolerated each other for the simple reason that they was all living in the same environment. They were sharing whatever they had, over the years it did form a camaraderie between them.

There is little or no documentation about the Fenian movement in York, although there was a strong Loyalist Irish organisation which met behind the King William. Legend has it that this is the reason why the pub was painted green. Owen Calpin explains,

There was meetings of different people and later on I found out it could have been the IRA, but they called 'em the Green Ribbon Club.

Hill's Yard with Biddy Quigley, granny of Jeff Quigley.

Thomas Abbot recalls the Irish people around him,

Some of those Irish women would never see me short. They looked after you, which was rather peculiar because I used to have to go the full length of Margaret Street to school and pass St George's, and there was times when I used to have to fight me way to school and fight it back. I had a lad that was a batman in the war years, Jeff Quigley, and he lived in Hope Street and we often laughed about it.

Albert Howard remembers that the English did integrate with the Irish, and enjoyed the social life together,

We used to sing out there at 12 o'clock on a night. All the street used to be out, when it was warm. They never used to go to bed, just sitting and singing, and smoking clay pipes. We sang all t'songs there was. I allus remember one, 'When Irish eyes are smiling'.

Many people comment on the amount of fighting in Walmgate, which was obviously linked to the amount of drinking. The Irish in particular certainly enjoyed a good fight. Dick Calpin, son of John and Lizzie, recalls two brothers,

Jackie and Tommie Harrison. They was the champion prize fighters of Walmgate. Every Friday, Saturday and Sunday night, they used to get 'abbreviated', take their shirts off in the street and they'd challenge anyone. Now I went up to 'em one night and I said, 'All right Tommy, I'll challenge you'. So he says, 'Right, Dick Calpin and me'll challenge any two in the street'.

The Yorkshire Evening Press of July 1924 reported that one of the Harrison brothers, on being arrested for being drunk and disorderly (his thirteenth charge), retorted, 'Well, I'm the boss of this street'. But Henry King remembers there was usually an element of gallantry,

There were a fair lot of Irishmen in those days, and fighting in Walmgate of a Saturday night. There'd be an old woman walking by and they'd stop fighting 'till she got past. 'Come on love, be quick' and they'd start fighting again. It wasn't like it is today, if a fella got knocked down they waited 'til he got up then had another go.

The only man who could stop a fight, apparently, was the priest. He had much more power than a whole force of policemen. Violet Quigley experienced this in her own house,

Every Saturday night we used to go out to watch fights. You wa'nt frightened in them days. They used to take their shirts off, just their trousers on and you'd see two brothers nearly killing one another. And next day you'd see 'em go to church then go sit in t'pub together.

And they were all frightened o't priest. I remember him coming here once. We had my husband's brother living here. We'd had our tea, and he was just eating a slice of bread and jam and I saw Father Ryan passing by. 'Oh,' I said, 'there's priest coming here.' Well my husband run in t'bathroom and Peter run upstairs and he still had slice of bread and jam in his hand. Priest come in and he said, right Irish like, 'Where are they?' I said, 'Well one's run in t'bathroom and one's run upstairs.' Anyway Jeff, my husband, come out o't bathroom, reckoning to dry his face wi't towel, 'Hello father', and Peter had to come down. He said, 'If you aren't at church on Sunday morning, I shall come up them stairs and drag you out of bed.' They went, don't think they dare do any other.

Olive Waudby remembers, as a child, being fascinated by the fighting,

Black Maria used to come down Walmgate on Saturday night, picking up drunks. There was the Irish club. A lot of drunks were turned out from there and I can remember with my brother and my sister sneaking out of the back way, when we heard an uproar, we'd go and we got into trouble for doing it. I wouldn't say it was just the Irish people who provided the drunks. All those pubs, they used to come from all over.

Of course, not all fights were between the Irish people. The Martinmas hiring fairs were often the time that grievances were aired between the farm labourers who were in the city for the day. The back streets and pub yards were usually the scene of many fights, which was a good way to settle disputes. Many of the labourers would come to be hired, have a

101

number of drinks, and if they ended the day with a good sparring, then they would go home to bed happy.

The other national trait seemed to be a love of singing, and Betty Thompson recalls,

There was a lot of pubs down there, full of Irishmen and they were real big men, they all had lovely singing voices. As a child in them days, you could hear them singing. Everybody was grouped together like a community.

Andy Waudby discovered how much the Irish people loved to hear songs which reminded them of home. This gave him a way of earning a few coppers. One day,

An Irishman pulled me up. He says, 'Son, could you sing a song for me?' I stood there on the pavement and sung 'Danny Boy' and there was about 30 summat people all round. Later I was sat on't flags and Alice and me had been swapping cigarette cards. It was a lovely summer's morning and this man comes up and says, 'Are you the one that sings in the streets, well I've got a job for you, you'll earn some money.' Well mention money and me lugs start flapping.

He took us up to the King William, it's in the Museum now. The doors was open and people were drinking. He says, 'Can you stand near that door, son?' This bloke come up with a mouth organ, he started playing, and he says, 'I want you to sing Molly Malone.'

I started singing and just as I was finishing it, this great big Irishman come out with a flat cap and one of them neckerchiefs. There was tears coming down his face and he took out his great big hand, (at the time I thought I was gonna be crushed) and he put it on my 'ead. Tears was rolling down his face, he puts his hand in his pocket and he brings this great big handkerchief out that was red with white dots on, he wipes his eyes, 'Thanks son'. And he puts his hand in t'pocket and still got me like that, trapped, and I daren't budge, and he gimme half a crown. So I took the half crown home to me mam, and Alice and me got a couple of taffee apples. It was wonderful.

The Lodging-Houses

Many of the itinerant Irish, who were passing through York in search for work, stayed in one of the lodging-houses. There were three main ones - Thackerays, (now Walmgate Pine), Saddlers (also at different times called Mahars and McQuade's), and the most famous, Kilmartin's, originally O'Hara's.

Ray D remembers Thackerays lodging-house, run by two maiden ladies, Caroline Thackeray, and her cousin Ada Walker,

You had to be very respectable to get in there. Irishmen, of course, but very quiet Irishmen. Every night they walked their Airedale dog up and down Walmgate. They had a shop front and all that was in the window was about half a dozen eggs. They was extreme ladies and they had to be extreme gentlemen to get in.

Violet Quigley remembers,

Thackerays lodging-house, two women ran that and it was spotless that place. Used to get Irish men in who'd nowhere to go and they'd sleep there and then go in t'tatie fields next day and work. Me mam once went there and she said it was beautiful and clean, all the beds was all lined up. And there was coffee house, that was a lodging-house, Saddlers. And she sold soup, used to go down with a big jug of soup, mebbe tuppence.

Caroline Thackeray eventually died in 1971 at the age of 88, in Oakhaven home in Acomb.

As an antidote to the waves of drunkenness spreading through Walmgate, the York Coffee House Company opened a building dedicated to temperance principles. Isaac Poad was one of the directors. The house comprised a refreshment bar, smoke room, kitchen and lavatory on the ground floor, with sitting rooms and seven bedrooms upstairs. The premises were opened by Lady Murray, who 'expressed the hope that it would be the means of promoting sobriety in Walmgate'. The coffee house (which later became Saddler's) was built in 1892. The York Civic Trust described it as 'an island of temperance in a sea of pubs'.

It continued in use until 1973, then in 1976 the Trust donated £5,000 to help convert the two upper floors into flats.

Since the book produced in 1988 by 'Walmgate and Friends' and its section describing life 'on the rope' at Kilmartin's, controversy has reigned. Terry Kilmartin whose uncle ran the house, and who lived there as a youngster, maintains that there was no such thing. Other people insist that it did exist. The story gave rise to a wave of correspondence in the local Press, mostly questioning how it was possible to sleep on a rope. A letter from a Mr Lack claimed that there was a rope, but it was used for the hanging of clothes, and that the story of men sleeping on it was pure invention, a myth which had grown up over the years!

Terry Kilmartin at Bowes Morrell House 1996

Terry Kilmartin feels strongly that,

It's all lies. There was three men that looked after the place, and they cleaned it and soaked it out. It was immaculate. There was a big massive table, about 12 foot long and four foot wide, there was three of them in there, two big gas ranges and a Yorkish range.

Kilmartin's and lane to St Margaret's Hall

They used to have the harvest, come for the potato picking. It got to be 'We'll go to Killem's lodging-house', and there was the Blue Bell across the road and Saddler's. Well they all took Irish men on. It was good fun, and they used to take it in turns cooking. And John and Fred, [Terry's uncles] if pensioners were there, they'd maybe be cooking chops and steaks and then John'd pinch a chop for one o't pensioners on t'corner, and then me dad used to go in to t'old people and give 'em some eggs. Me dad was a right generous old lad and with all t'hens we 'ad you see. In fact they killed two pigs and had 'em in the back of a van, and they got a tip off. One o't policemen told 'em, cos he was getting a ham for nowt and they rode round York for six hours in t'van till all t'coppers had gone.

Near t'Golden Barrel yard was a barber's shop called Patton's and they had sawdust down and spittoons for t'Irishmen coming in for a shave. Always reminded me of Tex Ritter in the cowboys, hit it from 30 yards away.

The O'Donnells

Eileen Brown's mother was one of the O'Donnell family who originated from County Mayo. They came to England in the 1850s, and by 1861

John and Margaret O'Donnell lived in St Margaret's Place with their family. Mayo, incidentally, was the birthplace of 40% of Irish immigrants in the 1851 census, and continued to be the most represented Irish birthplace, although it is the farthest county from Britain! Other counties appearing were Dublin, Galway, Roscommon, Sligo, Clare and Cork.

Eileen Brown remembers her mother,

lived in a passage in Walmgate and was married at St Denys's church to Len Holgate, me dad. I think he was of a bit better family, because me mother always said she was bought with black pudding and sausage. Grandma O'Donnell said to her, 'You don't fall out with 'im,' because he must have been providing the food.

Me aunt Emily used to walk from Rowntrees every morning to Poor Clare's convent on Lawrence Street, because they had services then. When the war was on, I was a driver at the railway and I used to deliver their unleavened bread. For a long time I didn't know what it was. In those days I knocked and they opened a little door, and I used to take this bread, Holy Communion I presume, in a big wicker basket.

Mrs Mary Booker's mother came from County Cork in Ireland, and left a place where she and her sister had had a pony and trap and a private education, to come to England, where their fortunes changed dramatically,

They let her go and look at this house. You opened a door and it was a big square, there was no sink in it, just stairs and a cupboard under them and the tap was in the street. Me mother took it and she was in it a fortnight and she didn't know anybody and she started in labour with me. So she went next door and knocked and an old woman come to the door. 'Come in love', I'll get you Mrs Barker, the midwife'. It was Saturday night just gone twelve o'clock and I was born.

Mrs Barker said, 'This baby won't live the night out'. I weighed four pound and half an ounce. The doctor came and he said, 'Go for a priest'. The priest came and said, 'What are you going to call the baby?' Somebody had a paper and brought it in. It had on, 'Lady Evelyn Mowbray in society wants a divorce', and me mother said, 'Call her Evelyn'. So the priest said, 'Merciful God, you can't have a baby and not call it a saint's name. Call her Mary Evelyn, the child won't live the night'. And Mary Evelyn's still here.

Many of the Irish who came were travellers, though a large number gradually settled down in York. York cemetery has many impressive monuments to traveller families, who are renowned for having lavish funerals. Friends and relatives come from miles around, and the wreaths are usually an incredible sight.

In the early days, travellers sometimes had problems integrating, but nowadays there is a National Association of Teachers of Travellers, which co-ordinates educational support for the children. It has links with the Showmen's Guild of Great Britain and the Society of Independent Roundabout Proprietors. Children who regularly move around the country are given a 'green card' which gives a brief record of the child's education.

One of the most expensive monuments in York Cemetery is a black obelisk made of Norwegian lavakite, the only example of this stone to be seen. It is dedicated to the memory of James Morrison, who is described as a hawker from Navigation Road. He died in 1918 in a caravan in Manchester. There is another tall monument of a woman in a shawl weeping, beside that of an angel. The inscription reads William Moore, china and earthenware dealer. The Moores were a well-known Walmgate family. One man whose family had always been travellers but who have settled in York, explained that every so often he still gets a strong yearning for the open road, for the freedom to travel during the day, and sit round a roaring campfire in the evenings.

The INL Club

The Irish community wanted a social centre of their own, and opened the Irish National League club off Navigation Road. There were also Irish bands in the area. John Sweeney remembers hearing about his grandfather, Patrick 'Porrick' Sweeney, who was born in Harper's Yard and worked as a glass-blower at Deuces glass factory in Navigation Road. The works would employ a taker-in who was responsible for bringing

107

beer into the factory for the thirsty men! Patrick was the leader of the O'Connor Band, and tradition has it that he would toss his baton over the top of George Street Bar and catch it at the other side during the marches. He was a big man and reputedly would dress in a policeman's uniform and go into pubs and quell trouble there.

Mary Booker recalls,

The INL club at the top of a passage. All t'Irish used to go in there, and there was some soldiers from Strensall. A fella there, and one of these soldiers got arguing, they beat him up this fella. And next day he was on a route march and he died. And a week after, there was loads of soldiers come down, they had bayonets and they were looking for these fellas. Then all the Redcaps, they'd got whiff of them, and they got 'em all back into Strensall without causing any trouble, but they were gonna kill the fella who killed the lad.

This old woman used to sit there with a pipe. She had about five lads and they had a band. On a Saturday night they used to say, 'Come on, let's have a singsong', and everybody'd be out dancing and singing. My mam was a right nice singer, she used to sing, 'I'll take you home again Kathleen' and they'd be crying, 'Sing it again, Kate, it reminds me of Ireland'. There used to be young Irish lads would come down and sing 'Danny Boy' and they'd lovely voices. And me mam'd give 'em a breadcake.

Violet Quigley recalls the INL club,

I used to go with me husband. There was no work and they used to go and sit in t'club during t'day and it was one of them old-fashioned fireplaces, brick round with like a big spout up. And they used to sit playing cards. Wa'nt drinking 'cos they wouldn't have the money to drink. Mebbe Saturday and Sunday night they had turns on. Or anybody could get up and sing theirselves. They'd all be together, a good old sing-song.

Owen Calpin enjoyed,

The concerts. Somebody banging about on a piano, they'd go up and sing their heads off. The concerts were very good and they used to entertain themselves, very rare they brought people in like turns and artistes.

Terry Kilmartin remembers that,

Gordon Calpin used to always sing the 12th Street Rag, and 'Goodbye', and they all got their hankies out, all t'women and they'd be waving, 'Goodbye, Goodbye, I wish you all a fond goodbye'.

The present INL club has been much extended and rebuilt. The original club was described as a tin hut. Today, as well as the main lounge, there is a snooker and billiards room, and a room with a stage for the entertainment. The lounge is adorned with photographs, and a glass case houses several cups and a large trophy for billiards. Today the club has between 250 and 300 members, not all of them regular attenders, but the actual Irish members can be counted on both hands. Yet the glass doors

INL Club Committee c1913

which separate the entertainments room from the bar have the shamrock and rose intertwined, which is one of the few remnants of the original club. It was completely refurbished in 1995 and now boasts fitted floral carpet, polished tables, games machines and potted swiss cheese plants.

6

Escape and Entertainment

The general consensus of the people who have lived in the Walmgate area at some time in their lives, is that it was probably the most exciting part of the city. The reason for this is the range and diversity of occupations, but the range of people who frequented the district. When asking anyone what they remember about Walmgate, the first response is something about the numerous interesting characters. It is these who make a place interesting, who give it life, and Walmgate has had more than its share of lively personalities.

Walmgate Characters

Thomas Abbot remembers one family,

Facing onto Walmgate, was a family called Claytons and Charlie Clayton was a big man in the scouts. He became assistant scoutmaster of Treasure House troop. Old man Clayton was a casualty from the war and eventually he couldn't get about. He used to have a pushchair, first of all he had a long bathchair and he steered it with one wheel at front. When he wa'nt about we used to get in it, and then they got him an ordinary chair with two wheels on. He was keen on t'gee-gees and he used to do a bit of running to get some money for one o't bookie's.

Mrs Dunnington remembers another character, well-liked by the local youngsters,

The Goody Priest. I don't know whether he was a catholic but he was a tall man, he wore a swallow tail coat and he had a Gladstone bag. As he passed he'd give you a sweet, he always kept them in the bag.

There were other characters who were not quite so popular. Violet Quigley recalls Mapp Snowdon, who sold newspapers. The children would tease him by shouting 'paper' and running away. He would then chase them, swearing and cursing, and even throwing papers at them,

And if you didn't buy any off him, he used to come out with all sorts, shouting and balling at you.

Harry Lovick remembers,

Somebody would say to him, 'I want a Sporting Pink, Mapp.' 'I haven't got one, I'll go and get you one.' So he'd go to Matty Myers and get one, yesterday's, and of course he wouldn't tell them. He'd give them it and get his penny and when they opened it, it was yesterday's.

Rubye Readhead recalls,

There was a chap who used to sell papers, he had an old delivery bicycle with a big frame and basket, and he used to put all the newspapers in that. He was quite a character, used to cycle up and down the pavements on this huge bike, it was like a monster. And he wouldn't think twice about slagging you off.

Many people recall the newsvendor Charlie Thornton, who always carried his newspapers on a bicycle. He died in 1960 aged 53 and there is a photograph of him in the Olde Starre Inn in Stonegate. Malcolm Ainsworth describes him,

He wore a long black overcoat and bike clips. He rode a bike, but he always had his hands in his pockets. He had a dog followed him. I was about 9 and my mother went to Leeds shopping and come back with a little dog. She had 42 pups in three goes. All her pups looked like her, small black and white mongrel, all barring one. It was a little weak black thing. We used to have an old iron range in our house, with an oven at side. Me aunt put it near there and fed it whisky and milk with a little doll's bottle and it survived.

One of these pups I give to my mate Alfie whose grandfather was Jenker Roe. Charlie Thornton used to go to their house with papers, and this dog started following Charlie. On a Saturday and Sunday night he'd be going round town and I'd see this dog after him, and Alfie who owned the dog, he'd be with me having a drink. And he shouted, 'Rex, come here' and dog used to just look and chase Charlie. The only time it went home was dinner time. And Alfie's granny used to say, 'That bloody dog, as soon as I put summat on t'floor, it gobbles it up and then it goes out again.' It followed Charlie for years.

Annie Pinder recalls her next-door neighbour who kept a donkey,

Donkey Dick, he mended wringer machines and we'd hear the donkey kicking, 'Ee-aw, Ee-aw'. I'm sure he had the donkey in the bedroom. His wife was badly, and he says, 'I think she's having t'bairn' so me sister took her to hospital. And when she got there, they sent for him to bring her back. He said, 'What's up with her?' and they said, 'She'd a good blast of wind and she's all right.' Wasn't half ignorant in them days.

And there was old Johnny Gray in Hope Street. He used to go round with a little tingalarie and they'd all come out dancing. 'Just a rose in a garden of weeds' and all these songs. That was the beginning of the First World War and then they said, 'Did you hear about poor Johnny's donkey, it's died, they're having a wake for it tonight'.

Street entertainers were a familiar sight and Violet Quigley remembers two,

Burlington Bertie used to come round singing and all t'kids used to follow him. And there was a funny little man and all he'd sing was 'Oh-ta-ra-ta-ta, oh-ta-ra-ta-ta, left right, left right, oh-ta-ra-ta-ta' and if you give him ha'penny or anything, he'd say, 'I didn't ask you for this, did I missus? If police come, you give me it, without asking'. And then lads used to get up to some right tricks. Jim Melvin, he's died now, he was right tall, and he got this policeman's helmet, I don't know where from, and a tunic. He was in this yard and his head was just peeping up and 'Oh-ta-ra-ta-ta' was singing and then all of a sudden, Jim bobbed up and said, 'What you doing?' Poor little man, he nearly died.
Ray D recalls Burlington Bertie,

who wore the bowler hat, very smart, with an umbrella. Very well educated. Used to walk round the city, straight as an arrow, immaculately dressed. Then he'd stop and put his hands up to his ears. He suffered from shellshock during the 1914 war.

Tom Rhodes recites the song which Bertie always sang,

> *I'm Burlington Bertie, I rise at ten thirty,*
> *And reach Kempton Palace about three,*
> *I lean on the rails, while there's 'orses for sale,*
> *You ought to see Donaghue watch me.*
> *I lean on the walling, while Lord Derby's yawning,*
> *He bids two thousand and I bid 'good morning',*
> *I'm Bert, Bert, I haven't a shirt,*
> *But my people are well off, you know.*
> *Everyone knows me from Smith to Lord Roseberry,*
> *I'm Burlington Bertie from Bow.*

Burlington Bertie

Jimmy Mullen remembers Old Walshy,

He used to have a walking stick and he'd come down t'street like Charlie Chaplin. Everybody knew him. We used to shout, 'Bang, you're dead, Walshy' and he'd just fall on t'floor and pretend to be dead. I think he lived in Kilmartin's.

There were others who unwittingly provided the locals with free entertainment, like Violet Quigley's neighbour,

There was a woman opposite us and her husband was a chimney sweep. They parted, fell out or summat. And she was in bed with this little fella out o't country, farm labourer or summat, on this Sunday afternoon. And all t'lads was outside fish shop, and her husband come down and he must have been wanting to talk to her. So Jim Melvin said, 'She's in bed with Jack. I'll get you a ladder and you can go up and see 'em'. He put the ladder up to t'window and he was nearly at top. And we was all stood laughing, and she must've heard him and come to t'window and was pushing t'ladder away. And he was dangling off top!

Dick Calpin recalls,

Crutchey Kilmartin, he had just one leg and he liked a little tiddley. Course you could get drunk on 1/6 then, you didn't have to have a pocketful of money.

Terry Kilmartin was related to Crutchey,

He was a cousin of me Dad's. He had one leg and he used to throw his crutch, a wooden one, into t'pub window. They used to throw him out and he'd chuck it through the window and then fight the coppers.

Not everyone thought ill of Crutchey, including Mary Booker,

They say bad things about him but he was a good fella and he had a cart, great big wheels on it and clean papers on it, and fish. He had a crutch and a right short leg, like a knee and a little bit of flesh, and a big boot on. He'd lean on his crutch and say, 'Bring out your dishes, I'll fill them with fishes, alive-alive-oh, alive-alive-oh' and everybody'd come out and he'd give you two or three of them for threepence.

114

Rubye Readhead recalls,

Every year there was a big Martinmas fair on St George's field. Our neighbour used to always take in two lodgers from the fairground people, and they were quite nice chaps. One night there was this big fancy dress ball at the Assembly Rooms. It's quite a select place, but these two decided they would go. They must have got off the fairground earlier than usual and went to the Assembly Rooms and weren't allowed in so they decided they'd go and have a drink. In those days there were lots of pubs on the way from the Assembly Rooms to George Street. You can imagine what state they were in when they were rolling down the street about midnight. One was dressed as a vicar and the other as a ballerina, and the racket they kicked up was out of this world. All the windows shot up and people came out, 'What the hell's going on?' Two men staggering down the road, a ballerina and a vicar! I don't think after that, she took any more lodgers!

Many locals mention Billy Wainman, the undertaker. Harry Lovick knew him,

He carried a tape measure in his pocket and when he saw anybody that wasn't looking very well or very old, he'd get it out of his pocket and measure them for the coffin, which I suppose didn't make them very happy.

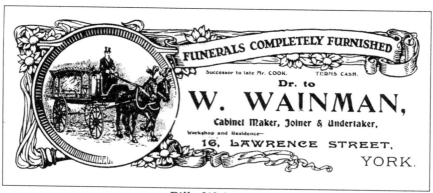

Billy Wainman

Mrs Booker also remembers,

Further down near the Bar there was Mr Wainman, undertaker, and he was only little and wore a top hat and black coat, swallow-tail. If you moved the collar, it used to shoot up. And these old women'd come out, 'Oh Billy I'm worried to death, I was thinking about when I die, and that lid come over, and probably I wouldn't be dead'. 'Well, what do you want me to do? I'm a busy man'. 'Oh Billy will you make sure, get a needle and stick it right through me and see if I move, Billy, and take the lid off and get the doctor to me'. 'All right Bridget I'll see to it'.

Less amusing is the tale of the Chinese Laundry at 137 Walmgate. Lim Shee-Jeng, the wife of Jeng Wey, died in April 1952, in tragic circumstances. Sheila White remembers it well,

I used to take my overalls there to be done. He had a little wife, she was like a little china doll. She only used to put her head round, and poor soul she looked so lonely and so fragile. That little girl never came out from her coming from China, I don't think she ever came through the front door. If she put her head round, he would be telling her, 'Go back and get your work done'. And she used to look at you and give you a little smile but never speak. And if he caught you smiling at her, or caught her with her head round the door, he used to clap his hands and back she used to go. Back to do the ironing and the washing. And she hung herself.

For women, life was often one long round of drudgery. There were certainly some remarkable women in Walmgate. Joyce Burnett's mother, for example,

She was a person who used to tell tea cups. She was very clever, everybody swore by my mother. They called her Maud Green, but she always got the nickname of Mitzy. People'd just come up and 'Can I come for a cup of tea?' and that was it. She'd know if anybody's coming or if certain people's going over the water, or there's a present on the way. Nothing bad. She worked in Hall's sweet shop at the top of Clock Yard.

As if looking after the family and working in the shop were not enough, Mrs Green was a bookie's runner and cleaned and baked for Sir Isaac Green.

Joyce Green and her mother

Ina Paterson recalls her great-grandmother,

Christened Ann Elizabeth, she was always referred to as Macey. She was the local midwife and also the caretaker at Navigation School, just off the back of Walmgate. She lived in the school house adjoining and when she was a midwife, she kept a box of clothing that people had passed on to her. Baby's bonnets or jackets or anything, they were kept washed and clean. And pieces of sheeting boiled and folded, to use as nappies. Often during the night the policemen would knock her up. 'Can you come, Mrs Boulton? There's a lady at Kilmartin's lodging house starting in labour'.

Macey Ann Boulton 1890s

So she would go across with her box. It was usually an Irish itinerant's wife that was having the baby. Next morning if she checked on 'em, quite often they'd up and gone, because they were walking round Yorkshire and into Lincolnshire, looking for work on the farms. And sometimes they paid her a fee, other times if they weren't well off, they'd bring her a bag of potatoes or carrots, which they'd earned from the farmer they were working for. These things in the box helped because these people travelled light, they walked many miles. There were no lifts and they hadn't money to pay fares so there was nothing there for the new baby coming into the world.

And she also used to make her own ointment, and people came from quite a wide area to buy her little pots for sixpence. Me mother had to go to Crows butchers across the road, and buy sixpennyworth of pig leaf, which is apparently the inner membrane of the pig's ear. Her grandma put it into the oven in a clean baking dish and rendered it slowly down. It made a thick white fat. On the outhouse roofs in the schoolyard there grew an awful lot of sempa vivum. It's a succulent in a rosette and it grows on rockeries, you don't need much soil. It grows copiously in the Mediterranean on roofs and walls. And they called it oozluk which is dialect for houseleek. She had a pestle and mortar, crushed it up and added it to this white fat, and it made a very good ointment which was used for nappy rash, and skin troubles, and it worked.

She used to make frumerty, traditionally round Christmas time, a big bowl of creeded wheat boiled up with milk and spices. Perhaps in some areas they laced it up with a bit of spirit.

Just after the war, there were some little cottages not far off St Margaret's church, and a pot hawker family lived in one of them. Their son must have been in t'army, and when they were all getting demobbed, across the front of the cottage they'd written in great big letters, 'Welcome home Alfie.' And that lettering was there for years afterwards and they were welcoming home Alfie Dear. He was quite a character because he used to go round collecting rags and bottles with a flat hand cart that he'd shove along. A knotted scarf and old overcoat.

Escapism

Life was hard, Sheila White notes how people needed some means of escape,

Everyone used to have crushes on the film stars and there was a cinema in Fossgate which is now Macdonalds furnishers. They changed their films Monday and Thursday. You got two films a week.

Marriage was the goal of most women. They wanted to be engaged by they were 20 or 21, and then marriage to follow and that's all they used to talk about. Some girls had a bottom drawer, they'd buy bits and pieces ready for their wedding. They didn't bother about careers. Everybody thought I was crazy when I used to go swimming or to Prunella Stack's health and beauty - I did that 'til I was 21.

The Public Houses

Walmgate has certainly become something of a legend because of its pubs, and claims as to the number have ranged from 20 to 50, to 'every other house', the number exaggerated as time has gone on. The peak probably came in the 1880s, after which time closer inspections were made, and at the annual brewster sessions (in August) many inns were forced to close, because the premises were unfit, or landlords allowed too much drinking after hours. In 1902, the York Licensing Justices reported on all the public houses in York, and listed 25 in Walmgate, plus four beerhouses. There were probably many other unlicensed beershops, which were little more than somebody's front room. The beershops largely died out after the First World War. They were pretty unsophisticated and often quite rough, so the magistrates tried to phase them out. It seems amazing that so many pubs could exist and make a living in the area. Much of the trade came from the cattle market as well as the farmers who journeyed into the city to the Parliament Street market to sell their produce. Leaving their ponies and traps in the pub yards, they would return later in the day and enjoy a spot of imbibing before departing for home. Tales are told of how it was often the pony rather than his master who remembered the way back.

The Brewers

Walmgate was also the scene of several brewers. Robert Hotham began his brewery and malting business in York in the early part of the 18th century. After his death in 1770, the business was continued in George Street by his widow, and later his son, Robert Welburn Hotham. Hotham's Court off George Street is named after them. By 1879, William Hotham and his nephew Newton were wine and spirit merchants, and owned many of the pubs in the Walmgate area. Avis, in his recent book,

'The Brewer's Tale' states that Hotham bought fifty pubs from James Melrose in 1879, having sold the brewery, maltings and ninety other inns to a triumvirate four years previously. The company became the Tadcaster Tower Brewery in 1882.

The TTB had its premises in George Street, leading through to Piccadilly, with stores for wines and spirits, and cellars for the beer. Many local people remember it, like Rubye Readhead,

We lived opposite and they had malt cellars with hops to make the beer, and little tiny windows at ground level, and you could look through and see the hops. I used to like the smell of them. The brewery went all round the street and down Dixon's Lane and ended in Piccadilly. Across in brewery yard was where they kept the crates of whisky. And during the war, the man next door to us, Mr Batters, he had the key. When the siren used to go, he'd open the big iron gates into the yard then the cellar where they stored the whisky, and we used to go in there to shelter.

And Malcolm Ainsworth,

Where there's a big gateway, Dixon's Lane, there was open windows with bars on. Used to put the grain and stuff, brush it out on the floor for it to ferment. I was only born a hundred yards off there, we were probably drunkards with impregnating all those fumes. We probably got a taste of it while we were still in our prams.

Ray D,

can recall as a kid all the old steam engines, sentinels and such as that, coming in on a night, steam blowing out of 'em and muck and smoke. On a morning you could hear 'em firing 'em up, oily rags being thrown on 'em, kept going. As kids we used to look down there and watch the men raking the hops 'till they were ready for making beer. That was interesting.

James (Jimmy) Melrose was born in 1828 and his family were fellmongers. He married the daughter of a Beverley brewer and in 1875 became a brewer, maltster, wine and spirit merchant in his own right. He was an Alderman and magistrate and involved in many York organisations, as treasurer for York County Hospital and School for the Blind, chairman of York Racecourse Committee and York County Savings Bank. In his spare time he was director of Yorkshire Insurance, Barclays Bank, York Gas Company and York Cemetery Company and then became Lord Mayor in 1876. He came to own many public houses in Walmgate, before his death at the age of 100 in 1929.

Noel Attree remembers Melrose's wine and spirit merchants,

It was just like a Dickensian place to walk in. There was a lovely counter, all polished woodwork. It was all written down beautifully, in longhand. Jimmy lived to a hundred. I remember me grandma asking him once, and he said, 'I always spend Sunday in bed, that's how I've lived so long'.

Reg Lambert also recalls Jimmy Melrose,

He lived in Water End in Clifton in some style, and my father used to do most of his painting and decorating. One Saturday morning he took me with him on the crossbar of his bike. I was possibly six at the time. Jimmy Melrose said, 'Come in here, son, sit on there'. [pointing to his knee] 'When you become a grandad, you'll be able to sit your grandchildren on your knee and tell them that you sat on the knee of a man who sat on the knee of Charles Dickens'. And such was the case. When the railways came to York it made it possible for Dickens to come to see his brother near Malton. Jimmy Melrose and his family went there when Charles Dickens was a guest, and then he was able to sit on Charles Dickens's knee.

When I was at St Lawrence's school, there was a lady who was known to our headmaster. She came to the school and she was 100. When she died, the top class of the school were taken along to provide part of the congregation at her funeral. It was memorable because very few children ever met a centenarian, but during my junior school years, I met two.

This woman must have been Elizabeth Blanchard, whose husband was the cousin of Jimmy Melrose. She died in August 1930. There were only four female centenarians between 1905 and 1930, and no other woman until the 1950s, so it was a rare occurrence indeed. David Poole's research shows that there were only three centenarians in York in the 1920s, compared with 67 so far in the 1990s!

The Crown Brewery (and London Spirit Warehouse) at 64 Walmgate was probably founded in 1828, as both an inn and a brewery, and managed by the merchant George Hutchinson. In 1848 the business was handed over to John Foster, who expanded trade considerably. During Foster's time there, two of his wives died, and a few years later the press reported the death of two more wives of John Foster, landlord of the Five Lions. A local wag commented that he made Henry VIII look like the perfect husband, but it was discovered that there had been two landlords of the same name in Walmgate. Foster died in 1871 and the business, run by William Todd, continued production until 1895.

As well as those mentioned above, some of the pubs had their own brewhouses in the yard, including the City Arms, which, in 1843, offered best gin for twelve shillings a gallon, very good gin for ten shillings and good gin for only eight shillings! The Clock, the Malt Shovel, the Red Lion and St Peter's Vaults all had their own brewhouses before 1900.

Today, Walmgate is left with only three pubs; the Spread Eagle, the Five Lions and the Red Lion, on the corner of Merchantgate.

The following pubs once existed on Walmgate itself and there may have been others:

Admiral Hawke, Admiral Nelson, Angel, Barrel, Bay Horse, Black Bull, Black Horse, Blue Bell, Brewer's Arms, Britannia, City Arms, Clock Inn, Crown Brewery Hotel, Duke of York, Five Lions, Full Moon/Barleycorn/Moon, Golden Barrel, Ham and Firkin, Hope and Anchor, King William IV, Lord Nelson, Old Malt Shovel, Prince of Wales, Queen's Head, Red Lion, St Peter's Vaults/Spotted Dog, Spread Eagle/Bricklayer's Arms, Three Cups and Windmill.

Off the main road, the Shamrock was located in George Street, presumably serving an Irish clientele, as would be the Hibernian in Fossgate. George Street also had the Foundry Inn. The Friendly Tavern was nicknamed Johnny-behind-the-church, as it was situated directly behind St Denys's church. The Square and Compass was in Hope Street, and its licence withdrawn in 1906. The Albert Inn in George Street closed in 1903, and a few years later the St George Tavern in Margaret Street closed in 1921. As well as the Lord Nelson in Walmgate, there was another Lord Nelson in Navigation Road, and the Admiral Nelson in Walmgate which was sold in 1809. The Black Bull on the corner of Walmgate and Merchantgate, closed in 1906, and in recent years it was an oriental craft shop, being replaced in Autumn 1996 by Dreams teashop.

The Angel Inn

Reg Lambert recalls,

Saturday afternoons there was always a tremendous number of people because there were more drunks in half a square mile there than anywhere else. It would be around half past four one week and we were walking home and all of a sudden I saw a man's boot and leg come out of a doorway, and a man shot across the road and went straight through the window of the Co-op on the corner of George Street. And inside there was an enormous display, big packets of washing soap. He went straight through the window and demolished this display, but when they dug him out, he was cut to ribbons with flying glass. He had been kicked out of the boozer by the landlord and straight across the road, his feet hardly touched.

Richard Sanderson was born at St Peter's Vaults, and remembers being afraid of the sound of the tanks in the attic as a child,

The horse drawn beer drays used to come up Willow Street. They lifted the trap door up and rolled the barrels down. There was a couple of rails down and chippings and straw at the bottom and just rolled 'em down into it.

The Phoenix

At the end of George Street, beside Fishergate Bar, is the Phoenix Inn, once called the Labour in Vain. Stan Leaf was landlord from 1953 to 1963,

Mondays and Thursdays, we were open till four o'clock in the afternoon. Market days it was hard going, instead of closing at three there was an hour extension for the market traders. No women allowed. A lot of women used to think they could get in and we were visited every market day by the police.

Used to get a lot of the Irish cattle men in. [One fell asleep] And he got in the toilet, and I thought the door's locked and I went outside and lifted it up, and he's sat on the seat and he'd put the bolt in and I'd to get a brush to put it back. He jumped up, 'I'm sorry, I'm sorry, I'm sorry'.

It was a popular pub. We'd a marvellous beer cellar, it came right up to the moat on the bar walls and in summer when it was hot, the temperature was ideal.

We used to get a lot of people coming in from St George's church and Saturdays we'd have a nice singsong in the back room. There was one chap, he was Irish and he used to sing some of the loveliest songs. And a little chap used to come in with one of these melodeons. We'd some good times.

Phoenix trip

Ray D frequented the place,

I lived in Osbaldwick then and used to come every other night to the Phoenix. Not for the beer. To have a yarn with the landlord, Billy Herbert. A great character, he could think up answers before you could think up questions.

Ted Ellison used to sell mussels round the pubs, always in evening dress with a carnation in his lapel, a basket over his arm, on a stand. He'd go into the pubs and you'd go and get your sixpennyworth of mussels. He was a real character, a very good boxer, came from Lancashire and lived with a family called Carney in Chapel Row. Went round all the pubs in York, only a little fella, very fit, two cauliflower ears. It was me birthday once and I invited a friend to the Phoenix and Ted brought us some oysters.

Terry Kilmartin recalls the singsongs,

At Christmas they'd be fighting like hell to get into t'Phoenix 'cos all t'boys used to go in there. Everybody had to sing or say a poem or a monologue, else you'd put summat in t'kitty. All the Nelson Eddy songs, and Irish songs mostly. They'd sing 'The Kerry Dance' and get everybody going. And then I used to sing 'Danny Boy' and 'Mountains of Mourne'. And they made a song up about the lodging-house, it had 36 verses.

The pub now has a picture of the lounge in the long-demolished Admiral Hawke Inn, which claims to have been Dick Turpin's hang-out. The Red Lion in Merchantgate is reputedly haunted by Turpin's ghost, another place where he may have hidden, before being caught and hanged on the Knavesmire in April 1739 and buried in the garden of the long-demolished church of St George of the Beanhills.

In 1973 the Phoenix went down in history as the setting for the television play 'Days of Hope' and eight years later was in the news again, this time because of the mis-spelt sign outside! The pub still has the old lamp over the gate which once led to a group of houses, Ebenezer Place. This small street was demolished in 1937 but the original sign remains.

The Newcastle Arms

Malcolm Ainsworth lived near a pub in George Street,

The nearest pub was the Newcastle Arms, which was about 30 or 40 yards away from our house. I used to go there for one or two old ladies who lived in George Street. Mrs Butterfield was about 80-odd, she lived across road and she used to sit on a little chair outside, and I'd go with a jug, probably on a Sunday. They'd say, 'Malcy, would you run and get us a jug of dinner ale?' You couldn't avoid spilling it so you had to always drink a little bit of froth off top. That would be my first taste of beer. I was probably about 8 or 9.

Women went in pubs but probably one or two o't old ladies still used to sit in t'passageway. It was more of a male territory. They didn't alter pubs in those days like they do now. The architecture of them, or the rooms. When you walked in, there was no carpet, it was probably terrazzo floors, a proper old pub, it smelt of beer. There was no food or anything. You just got a packet of crisps with a blue salt wrapper with it and that'd be it.

Lads such as us, we went in there and played darts and dominoes. The main bar had seats round it and cast-iron tables. They were always painted black and there'd be a couple of old chairs near t'bar, with wooden seats with spindle backs and arm-rests on.

Pubs were like that unless you went in somewhere like Betty's where it had probably 1940s style mirrors all over, and stipplework like in t'pictures, decorating and that, and a few fancy bits of gold band round it. Like cinemas, which were like palaces in those days. But the pubs were built like that because I don't suppose people spent a great deal of money in 'em, apart from on booze.

Mike Race remembers,

I used to drink under-age 'cos me father'd bring me a bottle of beer every Sunday lunch-time from when I was about thirteen or fourteen. I used to drink from about sixteen, seventeen, and he never minded. One pub you could get served in was the Newcastle Arms, a pub which had seen better days. I'd go in there when I was an altar boy, from church on a Sunday night, a few of us used to go across.

One man remembers,

There was a lady who the boys knew as Mucky Margaret, when I was about fourteen or fifteen, who had the reputation for being a prostitute. I certainly remember hearing this noise down an alley one evening and seeing her leading this drunken Irish bloke and counting some money. I would assume it was for

128

services rendered. But she was a pretty unsavoury character and she was an alcoholic I think. She was the only one I actually knew who would perform services.

The Red Lion

The Red Lion in Merchantgate claims to be the oldest pub in York, along with the Black Swan in Peasholme Green. The foundation stone is of the 13th century, and the pub has been altered and renovated many times over the years. Noel Attree lived there, when his grandmother was the licensee in 1914,

Singing room was for ladies and gentlemen. A lady wouldn't go in on her own. There was a room which was known as the dram shop, there were wooden seats and the bar. In the front of it there was a trough of sawdust and spittoons. And that was usually for lads who'd been employed in the building trade or in the fields. There was a little window, jug and bottle department it was called.

Summertime they'd have a big jug and sit out on the steps, talking in the summer weather. If I was going past, I've heard Mrs Cook say, 'Do us a favour, Noel. Fetch us threepennorth of dark mild and ask John to give it a long pull, will you?'

A long pull means you give them a bit extra. Then you went through another door into what was the tap room. You could play darts or dominoes, cards wasn't allowed at any stage.

In the singing room there was a draught excluder, and piano was at the back of there. She employed a pianist did grandma, during the season. Wintertime mostly, because in those days, you'd get these people from the music hall. They were out of 'The Stage' magazine. You put an advert in there and got quite a lot of applications. The lady was paid of course, she had free board and lodge. Fella called Tom Machen used to sing, he had red hair. After the First World War, he'd sing, 'When the Sergeant Major's on parade' and 'Roses of Picardy'.

But then they came down on singing for some reason. Mr Woolnough was the Chief Constable and the Chief Inspector was a man called Williamson. A singing

room had to be a certain cubic capacity and if it didn't, then you couldn't sing, you had to apply for a licence.

Underneath the window where I was born, there were two stone steps or slabs. I'd go about half past ten on a night with two pint bottles, open this door and put them at back of the stones. You went to bed and next morning, they were still there but empty. I'm almost sure it was the police who had them.

One old Irish lady used to come in the dram shop, which was the Irishmen's place. She'd sit right up again the counter on this wooden seat, and have a pint of beer. We used to sell clay pipes those days with a longish stem, and she'd nip it off and break the stem in half. She used to have a piece of plum tobacco, and cut it off with a knife, roll the bacca in her hands, fill her pipe and light it.

There was another very distinctive looking lady. She used to come in and have a pint and smoke a woodbine. She'd stand by the fireplace wearing a very bright yellow blouse and she'd long, brass earrings and raven black hair, parted in the middle and a bob at the back. Very striking.

Noel also tells a story about another pub, the King William,

It was the talk at the Red Lion for a month or two. A fella walked in on a Thursday night into Alf Keech's. He had an old fashioned grey checked suit, lovely raincoat and old gladstone bag. He walked to the bar and he says, 'A whisky and soda, landlord, please'. Then he says,'Will you have a drink with me, I've done very well today'. So Alf has a drink. Then, 'Would you like a drink, lads?' and up they come, four or five pints of beer. 'Good health to ye, sir' he says, and gives Alf a five pound note. And he gets four pound, sixteen and sixpence change. He says he's in agricultural machinery and on his way back to Birmingham, but just has time for one more round. And he changes him another five pound note.

About half an hour later there's a tap on the window. Alf lifts it up, two fellas there. Crombie coats and bowler hats. 'Mr Keech?' 'Yes'. 'C.I.D. I've got a list here of spurious five pound notes, I'd like to have a look at any you've taken'. They look at the notes. 'Yes, they're both on here, I'm sorry Mr Keech but by law we'll have *to take them. We'll get this fella, don't worry, we'll be straight back, we'll get him on the train'.*

So he waits for a week and then he walks in to the old police station in Clifford Street. 'I'm going to see Mr Woolnough, the Chief Constable'. Straight up the stairs, doesn't bother to knock. 'Where's my tenner? I want me two five pound notes back'. The penny dropped, of course. They were all three of them in it together, and what a lovely trick!

Today the Red Lion still has the original red and blue floor tiles which were put in by Noel's grandfather. Instead of all the separate bars, there is now one big room, with the bar in the centre. The clientele is mostly young, though there are a few older people. There are several additions which were not there in Noel's day, such as the stereo jukebox, provision of meals and the chocolate condom machine in the ladies' toilet!

The Five Lions

The first mention of this inn is in 1805, and the licence was transferred several times by 1842. In 1871 it was well-established as a place offering stabling for 50 horses and standing room for 70 more. The landlord, Henry Schofield, also had horses and traps for hire.

Ray D remembers it in the 1930s,

Peter Veitch, the ex-Scots Grey, he was the landlord when I was round there. He was also gamekeeper for Lord Halifax. We got on very well with him, he had a constant clientele. His daughter Peggy Seago ran it after he died.

Today the pub is very much a male domain, and the evening I visited it, all the customers were glued to Sky TV to watch Henry Wharton box his way to victory. In a crowded pub, the only females present were the barmaid and myself.

The Lord Nelson

In the 1870s, the Lord Nelson was well-used by farmers coming into the city. Like the Five Lions, the inn had stabling, though only for forty horses, with space for sixty standing on market days! Meals were provided every Saturday at 1.30pm and fortnightly on Thursdays (cattle fair days) at one o'clock. As well as offering ale, porter, spirits and wines, they were also dealers in hay and straw.

Nearly a hundred years later, Vera Lyall was landlady at the Lord Nelson from 1957 to 1962,

We got a lot of country people who were very nice, from Naburn and Stillingfleet and all that area. They used to bring you big baskets of home-grown vegetables.

There was a little second-hand clothes shop and a big family lived there, the Tunstalls. They were travelling people. They used to come in. Mrs Tunstall's sister lived higher up, where George Street is. Tommy Vickers was her husband. If any of 'em was having any carry on, he went straight up to them. And he was the boss.

His wife said to me one Christmas time, 'Call in when you go to the [Co-operative] Stores. I want to give you a drink and a piece of cake.' So I went through the shop and into the back and I've never seen anything so beautiful. All the crystal and pottery, chinaware. Only a small room but absolutely full of it.

If they had any wakes, we got them. After the funeral these women used to get in the room, and start doing 'Knees up Mother Brown'. All their frocks up and you could see their underwear. It was a right do when anybody died.

One time this lad brought in a newspaper parcel, a silver teaset, and put it on the counter, this was at a lunchtime. I thought, 'Hello, there's something funny here.' Then I looked in the cream jug and there was all congealed milk in the bottom. Turned it round and it was some hotel, I forget which one it was now. He'd pinched it. So I said, 'Take that out. I don't want it'.

When the Lord Nelson closed in 1982, it became the area sales office of Bass North East in summer 1984.

Robert Kay, known as Grandfather Kay, was a bootmaker at 56 Walmgate, who became a magistrate in 1912. Kay, a man with a strong social conscience, was a JP, freeman, precentor at the Wesleyan church, and instrumental in raising money for the new County Hospital. A staunch teetotaller, he became known for keeping a diary about the pubs and bad behaviour in the street.

Vera Lyall outside the old Lord Nelson 1996

Mike Race's great-grandfather was the tenant of the Britannia Inn in the latter years of the 19th century. The place seems to have deteriorated from the 1830s when it was the meeting-place of members of the Loyal Ebor Lodge. Robert Kay's diary described one particular night in 1882 when 'not less than forty militia men with a lot of low Irish girls...did as they liked all over the house...they could not be controlled'. He also mentions that a few years later, the two daughters of the house had not been in the place a year before they became prostitutes. Kay objected to the licence renewal so it was refused in 1900 and the pub closed.

In those days before the turn of the century, life could be pretty rough and things went on which wouldn't even happen today, in terms of public morality. I think the Britannia was a place where girls of ill-repute and soldiers gathered. There was a lot of that sort of thing in Walmgate but I think it was cleared up by the time of the First World War.

The Spread Eagle

The Spread was one of the smallest of Walmgate pubs, with stabling for only five horses. The first licensees were the Daltons in about 1867 when Mr Dalton merged his barber's shop with the pub. Robert Kay reported that Mr Dalton 'was not very law-abiding, he would supply drink as long as they could stand to drink it'. The place traditionally attracted a lot of travellers, and in 1902, advertised that 'two hawkers' vans are allowed to stand in the yard most of the year'. Bass North auctioned off the pub as a free house in 1977 and it is now acclaimed as one of York's finest places for real ale. In 1990, Shylock's restaurant opened upstairs and is often featured in the 'food and drink' columns of the local press. The lunchtime clientele tends to be mostly local business men and women.

The Off Licence

Sheila White ran an off-licence in Walmgate from 1965,

That was a full off-licence with pumps and I used to sell draught beer, draught cider, wine and sherry by the pint, with spirits and everything. You could get what you got in a pub, but it was over the counter and I had a small outlet for groceries. I was there for about 2 years and then they put the CPO [Compulsory Purchase Order] on them because it was going to be a redevelopment area.

It was a lovely building, big palatial place. There was two windows, one in Walmgate, one in Albert Street. We had a side entrance for the private house, a large kitchen, a big pantry with stone flags, hooks to hang the bacons and things up. I had a farmhouse table in there, you could seat about 12 round it and still have room to move. Then there was a beautiful wide staircase to go upstairs, with walnut banisters. That went up on to the first floor and I had a lounge up there.

We had seven bedrooms altogether. I had a door at the side, you went down into a huge cellar. The cellar had been re-bricked inside because it was the air raid shelter during the war. And we used to have parties down there. We had outbuildings outside and I kept my bottles and beers in these. From the side of the building there was a big door, and it was one of the fan-shaped windows above the door, a bit like 10 Downing Street. In the front bedroom was an Adam fireplace, with little cherubs and everything, beautiful.

Sheila White and son David at Walmgate Off-Licence

We sold soap powders, mops, brushes, buckets, bowls, tea, sugar, flour, sauce, things that people would forget. Handkerchiefs, and stockings, socks and little fancy coloured aprons, yellow dusters, washleathers. I used to get them off Tommy Vickers, a nice family in Walmgate.

When we were there, it was quite good. Good wages and people had moved out of the old properties that were ramshackle and were all in the new estate, Navigation Road, Rosemary Court. They were all new properties and that uplifted them. Some of the people worked at the Tadcaster Tower bottling sheds, down in Long Close Lane and down Lead Mill Lane and they lived in brewery houses in George Street. When I was a girl it was very rough down there and there was some very poor people. But they'd sort of overcome that, it was when they pulled out all old Walmgate, and built the new properties.

I didn't know anyone that was not in good circumstances when we were there. There was one or two men slept rough in Poad's Yard, men that were just hard on their luck. They used to come in my shop and if we'd had a joint or if I'd done a honey gammon, and there was a bit left, the thick end of it, I would say to them did they want it. But they never took advantage and at the end of the week, they would put a copper on the counter and say, 'Buy that little girl some chocolate'.

Jimmie Swales was funny. He was a traveller. He used to come in every morning and he could make you laugh. He said to me, 'I've a mobile bed you know. My bed's on wheels. I'm going to bring you it and show you it.' It was one of those old wicker basket spiral chairs with four wheels and he wheeled it into the shop. Poor Jim, he was in my shop one morning and he died at night. He was only young, he wouldn't be 50. They came from near and far, there must have been 500 followed him, came from all over and I left my shop door open. I stayed up until 12 because it was summer and they were all sat outside on the pavement drinking. When I got up next morning, there wasn't any bottles - everything had been taken outside, packed up, and there was all the money on the counter. I took about 300 and odd pound that day, and they drank for three days.

I went to see him and he was like a king laid out in state. He was a nice man, he always wore a doeskin fedora. Used to give me a little patter as he came in, take his hat off, do a little dance.

The Malt Shovel

The site of the Malt Shovel was excavated in 1986. In 1978, in the carpark of Kay and Backhouse, a piece of mosaic had been discovered showing two crossed spades and the sign 'Brett Brothers. Ye Olde Malt Shovel', (Brett's were the brewery). The mosaic is now in the Castle Museum.

Maureen Aspinall remembers,

I'd gone to t'fish shop at corner, only two doors off and I remember opening the back door to go down this passage and this bloody great policeman stood in front *of me. I screamed, I was frightened to death. Me mother come running out and he says, 'It's all right, I'm only watching the pub'. All the drunks used to come out, I used to hang out of the bedroom window watching 'em fight. Used to be loads of fights, especially outside t'Malt Shovel. We thought it was great to see all that going on.*

Ray D remembers meeting his wife there,

She was looking after the pub while the landlady was on holiday with her husband. Forty one years ago I walked into the pub, said 'good morning' to her and I'm still saying it to her.

The one that women used was the Clock Inn, directly opposite St Denys's church. And there was a small passage with seats round it and an aperture in the wall, and that's where the women used to sit on a lunchtime. Glass of beer and a yarn then back to whatever they had to do in the afternoon. I don't think they particularly went for the glass of beer because they couldn't afford it, they went for the yarn.

Terry Kilmartin remembers the Golden Barrel yard which was full of pigsties and horse boxes. It took up the whole length of Margaret Street, and they used to let the pigs have races from one end to the other, having bets on who would win. The pigs were mostly black and white saddlebacks. There was also, at one time, bare-knuckle fighting and a fee was payable on the door.

The Brown Cow

The Brown Cow in Hope Street made the news when it took part in a radio darts match against the Ark at Maidenhead in April 1939. At that time the pub had six darts boards. It is also well-known for pool and dominoes.

Violet Quigley remembers the original pub, before the extensive alterations of recent times,

Me mam used to go in. It's the same outside but when you get inside it's different. In them days when you went through t'first door, there was what they called the best room. Another one at other end was where all t'men used to go. And all t'women used to sit in t'passage.

Violet and Jeff Quigley outside the Brown Cow

Olive Waudby remembers,

There was a man opposite and he used to do all our house painting. He was a jovial man and his wife was a nurse. She used to trot out with her jug when he was out at work, he knew she liked a bit, but I don't think he knew she went every day. She'd go with this jug to the Admiral Hawke and get it at the counter.

138

Often when pubs closed, the licence would be transferred to other premises elsewhere in the city. The Clock Inn, for example, closed in 1957 and its licence transferred to a new house on Cornlands Road. The Full Moon had its licence transferred in 1938 to premises on Huntington Road, probably the Bridge Hotel. The King William IV closed in 1956, and its licence moved to a new pub on the Chapelfields estate. The frontage of the King William was removed to the Castle Museum, where it also includes parts of one or two other pubs including the Newcastle Arms. The Brewers' Arms had closed in 1906 and compensation awarded. At the end of the 19th century, the licensee had been Matthew Myers, perhaps a relation of the well-known Matty Myers.

Long Close Lane with Brown Cow

Sport

The Walmgate area was one where sport was predominant, and many kinds took place there from cricket to club swinging!

Swimming

Albert Howard learnt to swim,

Down below Doves's iron foundry, Piccadilly. I had a grandmother lived there, she'd say, 'If you want to go in that river, blinking well put your clothes in here, just go over t'wall, nobody'll be any wiser.' And I did do, that's where I learnt my swimming. I used to go in every day I could. Used to swim on one leg while I got going and I got meself going in eight weeks. I was only about eight or nine. I was a terror at times, in warm weather there'd be a load go in there, in t'Foss. We used to dive off Castle Mills bridge, we got a crowd round and police didn't like it. I'd only t'wall to go over and to me granny's, I was away. Before I was 14, I went in the schoolboys' championship for York and won it. I got one of these leather bags what doctors carry about, it was beautiful. I won a cup, it was a lovely trophy and I kept it 'cos we'd won it eight times. I didn't win it eight times, somebody else had beforehand. I won it 1922 or 3. Me sister said, 'Ooh look at him, we didn't think he had it in him.' I said, 'Nobody teaches me anything, I do it meself'.

Dick Calpin, as well as being captain of the school rugby team in 1922, and a member of the York Rugby League 'A' team when they won the Yorkshire Senior competition in 1931, was also a swimmer,

I was the schoolboy champion at 50 and 100 yards. The championship was solely for breast stroke up to the year that I won it, and they changed it from breast stroke to free style.

It was for the whole of York, swam in St George's Baths. We learnt to swim in the Foss, I was seven years of age when I first went in. We'd congregate in the summertime and there was a place at the end of Navigation Road next to Leetham's Mill where we could strip and just go in, until the police came. Where the electricity place is, the warm water came underneath Foss Islands Road and we'd swim around there. We'd be swimming along and suddenly a dead cat would float by!

We used to dive into the river and one time I went too near the bottom and I've got a mark on me chest that's still there. I didn't tell me mother until she came to

*wake me one morning to go to school and my shirt must have been open, then she
saw the scar and I had to tell her.*

*I remember Mr Martin our headmaster, sending for me to his own home, to have
a chat and encourage me to do well for the school in the swimming sports. He
died two days later.*

Phoenix Juniors

Boxing

Although fighting was very common in the streets, boxing as a sport was
also popular.

Owen Calpin's uncle James, the steward at the INL,

*was a boxer. He fought Iron Haig at the North of England championship in
Middlesbrough. Jimmy beat him and his supporters carried him shoulder-high in
triumph back to Walmgate. They had a little hall up the side of St George's
church, where they fixed up a ring and they fought there.*

Ray D also remembers boxing,

At the bottom of Margaret Street there was Yorkshire and Lancashire Boot Repairers. At the other side was Ted Beesons upholsterers and they used to train boxers in the back. Arthur Dale was the man that trained, he turned out to be a very good boxer. Poor lad got killed on a motorbike. Another lad who trained them was Vince Capaldi of Capaldi's ices. They'd a ring up in the old lofts. Every place had an old loft and also at the back of the Blue Bell in Walmgate, Mortimer's trained boxers.

Terry Kilmartin recalls,

There was a fella who could box like Joe Louis and dance like Fred Astaire. This fella was six foot six with red hair and the first time I met him I was eighteen, and I was doing judo at the time and rugby and me dad and me uncles had been drinking together and they must have thought, 'I wonder if our lads can look after theirselves?'

I got out of bed and flew down to t'lodging house and they said, 'There's a fella in there and you can't get in for him, he's hitting everybody and can you sort him out?' Me cousin had been brought from South Bank, so we went in and I come flying out like John Wayne. They'd two swing doors, he hit me and I went through t'door. I says to me cousin, 'Now go in and tackle him', and I went in and I chopped him behind t'ear and dropped him. He put him in a builder's van with a low back, took him on t'racecourse and dumped him.

He was back in half an hour and he says, 'Was it you that hit me? Let me shake your hand'. And we was great pals and we was always sparring, he was showing me all the dirty tricks, which I knew actually. And he could dance like Fred Astaire, he was brilliant, you know the Irish dancing. Big John Henry they called him. They run the boxing back of the Spotted Cow. We used to carry the water, get in for nowt.

Rugby

Malcolm Ainsworth,

used to play for Heworth, which is still on t'go, but it was a bit out of town. I signed on for t'Imperials with Stan Flannery when we were at school and we got in trouble because we were playing for St George's school and for York Boys together and then we had trials for Yorkshire Boys and we signed on for t'Imperials which was an amateur team.

I went with Terry Kilmartin. I think he should have been playing the day I went to Heworth with him, I think he was injured and I only went to watch, I was 15. And it was open age and they were short so I played in t'front row. I'm almost certain I scored a try, somebody probably gimme a good pass. But I remember who was in t'front row and two of 'em really sorted me out. I finished up with concussion or summat. It was a baptism of fire.

Other Sports

Mrs Olive Waudby remembers rather more sedate sports.

I and my sister were friendly with some people called Bowes, they had a bungalow at the back of the Working Men's Club in Tang Hall Lane. We used to go to play tennis with them and my sister said, 'Your court doesn't do anything, why don't you let it out?' So we rented it for St Denys's tennis club.

They had a cricket club, because our friends have given many a cricket supper, preparing all the stuff, trifles and so on. We used to get them from Miss Hawksby, she cut ham on the bone and sometimes we'd do rabbit pies. They played on the Knavesmire and sometimes on the Low Moor on Heslington Road.

I think the reason we got people interested in cricket, both HF Storey and his son Arthur from the Army and Navy store, belonged to the Revellers cricket team and they were responsible for getting St Denys cricket team together. The Revellers was a well known York team, did awfully well all over the place. Always used to be turned out in white smart flannels.

St Denys' School cricket team 1923 with Stan Lea

St Denys' School sword dancing team 1923

Stan Lea was a sportsman as a boy, and was captain of St Denys's cricket team, who had their pitch at the Beeswing on Millfield Lane, as well as participating in inter-schools competitions in rugby and football. In 1923 his school won a certificate for the schools competition in sword dancing, and the cricket cup for the first time in 1923. He remembers competing against St George's,

They were very friendly, St George's. And Jeff Quigley, he was a smashing half-back. He was only small but he could run and he was very clever, took some catching.

The INL club (see also chapter 5), was the scene of several sports victories, mostly indoor sports. The club won the National Billiards Championship Cup in 1929, 1931, 1932 and 1938. They have also won the President's cup for bowling, and cups for being the Cribbage League winners 1974-8. The club carries on the Walmgate tradition, with indoor games such as snooker, darts, whist, pool, cribbage, indoor bowls and billiards, and participates in leagues and team knockouts between September and April.

Entertainment

Despite the struggle to survive, an ever-present problem, the people of Walmgate and perhaps the children in particular found innumerable ways of keeping themselves amused. The lack of money seemed to make no difference, they could still explore other possibilities.

Stan Lea believes that life was much livelier than it is today,

You'd always somewhere to go. There's nothing to do today, they're bored. We'd go down to Dennis Street and have a bonfire, and sparklers, all such as that.

They really enjoyed theirselves, and in the streets there was a lot of gambling going on. And I've played jink. You made a ring on the pavement, there was some money on t'ring, put your pennies on and go for them, and if they jink the penny, you took it off.

145

Members of Boys' Club, outside Co-op in George Street,
once the Albert Inn, 1930s
Back row: Frank Oakley, Routledge, Albert fawcett, Jimmy Kelly,
Jim McAndrew, ?, George Driscoll
Front row: Joe Hennegan, Tommy Gallagher, Sonny Cargyl, Bert
Stockdale, Joe Beddingham

Annie Pinder also enjoyed life in Walmgate,

*When we was young we'd climb the walls and come into Navigation where there
was swings. We used to play shops down there, with glass for silver and gold.
There were always big lumps of slab, old stone. And there was nicks and grooves
in them.*

*I didn't have no toys. I used to have a piece of stick and I'd get paper and wet it
then squeeze it together, wrap it up and tie a band round and play rounders. The
skipping rope was from orange boxes, in them days they used to come in a carton
and there was a divider in 'em, wrapped round with a piece of rope and that's
what we used. The legs used to be scratched off you. This friend of me sister's,
Luke O'Hara, come down at Christmas to have a drink with us and he gave our
Winnie and me sixpence each. Shops were open till all hours o't night so we run*

down to Sellars's Yard and there was a shop there and we got these two dolls and they was all sawdust legs. They had wax feet, wax arms and wax faces and ooh we thought they was lovely. I went home and took the doll to bed. Next morning when I got up, I'd no doll left. With me being in bed, the wax had run into it, and I was sat crying.

Violet Quigley remembers,

When it was voting day we allus used to go to St Denys's schoolroom. We had a big red tablecloth and we used to run round t'streets wi't banner up in t'air, singing, 'Vote vote vote for Mr Butcher. You can't vote for a better man. Mr Butcher is the man and we'll have him if we can. And we'll chuck old whoever-he-was over the wall.' But Labour never gorrin in them days, they were all conservative, you were wasting your time.

We was in George Street me and Mary, and there was a shop just at top, a newsagents called Ashtons. If you saw a little toy, you paid a penny a week and you got it at Christmas. We was looking in but it must have been warm weather 'cos she got stung with a bee, a wasp or summat, and she run home screaming at top of her voice. Would only be about 9 or 10. So I'm running with her and when we got in t'house, I says, 'She's got stung with a wasp'. Her dad says 'What was you doing?', so I says, 'We was only looking in Ashtons.' He give her one smack across face and he says, 'Serve yourself right for looking in ashtins'!

And t'lads used to be gambling in t'cut, and every so often, t'police used to raid 'em, car used to come down Long Close, one down Hope Street, and they met at both sides. They used to have lookers-out to see if any coppers was coming and when they got the wire that there was some coppers on the go, they'd run. And they'd run in anybody's house and coppers used to chase after 'em. One old woman, Biddy Langan, said she was going down to t'police, she'd just got all her dinner out and puddings was up in the air, 'cos they was all running through the house.

We used to go to t'Electric. There was an old woman playing the piano and if cowboys was running to chase somebody, ooh she banged like owt on t'piano. And when it was a love scene, she went right quiet.

147

Thomas Abbot recalls,

In Hungate, you were going into foreign territory and you didn't tread. At top of Walmgate, on the left hand side there was a yard and in there was quite a well-known boxer, Boxer Merryweather. As a kid I used to play with his son. I didn't go much out of the yard, even at that age we learnt very quickly. There was only passage into the yard and as little as we were, we could defend that yard. When we went outside we realised we were weak so we stayed where we were safe.

Andy Waudby always found plenty of ways to occupy his time,

Used to go to Robson's rag and bone place and you could get a good pair of wheels for barrers for threepence or a tanner. We'd go into Park Grove or Haxby Road into the dustbins, get a few jam jars, wash 'em in the yard and then go up to Robson's. And then there was Gallons's shop at the bottom. We used to go in there for broken biscuits and bacon pieces. The chap there was very good. 'Any broken biscuits?' 'Just a minute son, I'll get you some.' He'd lift the lid and put his hand in and he'd get the biscuits and crush 'em, and put 'em in a bag for me. 'How much do I owe you mister?' 'Oh it's all right son, away you go'.

At bottom of Coppergate was Hooks's gunshop and fishing shop. If we had a bit of spare money we went and bought some stink bombs, it's God's honest truth, and we used to walk in between the crowds and you'd see these big bullies, Blackshirts, and we used to go and stand at side of 'em and drop stink bombs.

And then there was the time that Alice and me and Georgie Pearson, we were in Navigation Road and we came across an old chap sat on the flags rubbing hisself down. And there was this old three-wheeled bike on one side, tipped over. And he was cursing and ripping at this bike. He says, 'You can have it'. So Georgie and me got the bike, stood it up, there was no brakes, no mudguards on it. It's a good job it was a quiet day in Walmgate. Georgie got on the seat, I stood on the back with my hands on his shoulders. We pushed it off and we started going down Walmgate and one of the wheels got fast in the tramlines. It was a devil of a job, and Georgie couldn't get out and we gathered speed and just hoped there was no tram coming. I thought when we got to the bottom we were gonna stop or we'd go round with the tramlines, but instead the bike went straight on to t'bottom of Foss Bridge and we finished up in the gutter near Backhouse's.

Once Alice and me was going up Walmgate and we passed this lady with an oblong basket with a big handle and she stopped in front of t'Spread Eagle. She says, 'Can you look after this basket and I'll give you tuppence?' She disappeared into the Spread Eagle. Next minute she comes out, she had arms like ham shanks, and she had this little bloke by t'scruff o't neck and she's dragging him out. And he's a bit canno. 'I don't wanna go', he says. Anyhow she dragged him out and she was bending down to get the basket up. He started to turn round and go back into the pub and she reached down and there was a chicken, it had been plucked but it had its legs on. And she picked this chicken up and took a big swipe at him. Well he ducked and I was stood there and I got hit wi't chicken. Well she wa'nt satisfied with that and she started bombarding him with eggs. Well I got hit in t'face because he kept ducking and I kept getting hit with eggs. I had egg right down my neck. And in t'finish she grabbed him, picked the basket up and proceeded up Walmgate. 'Eh missus you left your chicken.' She says, 'You can have it, son'. So I took it home and we had a rare treat.

Dick Calpin enjoyed another spectacle,

There was a slaughterhouse down Speculation Street and when we left school we used to go down there and they had the beast in one section. The butcher Dent put the rope round its neck and put it on a hook on the floor and we'd help to pull the beast out. Then he used to hit it on top of the head.

We waited until they skinned it, drew the innards out of it and the eyes and the water used to come out. And when they killed the pigs, they'd scald them in boiling water and then scrape them. They'd bring them out and lay them on a of table, then they had a long cane and put it through the brain. That was our entertainment.

Stan Cowen also visited the place,

On a Monday and Tuesday after the market, the doors were open and we used to just stand and look at this grizzly scene. But in those days we took it as part of life's very rich pattern. This was life, seeing the bullocks being held by the ropes through a ring to the floor while the man used a pole axe to kill 'em.

There was a blacksmith's and I think they called it Bradleys. And you could go by there and see the horses being shod, you could smell it before you got near it, from when they used to put the irons on the horses hoofs.

A big event for adults and children alike was the Eclipse of the Sun which took place on the 29th of June 1927. The local Press described it as 'one of the most spectacular events in Nature's repertoire of pageantry'. The eclipse itself came over the country in a belt, and York was just outside the immediate path. But it was still possible to see the eclipse from a high vantage point, and the Bar Walls was the best place to be on that day. Men and children lined the walls at the bottom of Walmgate waiting to witness the spectacle. Interestingly, in photographs of this scene, the women are few and far between. They were probably far too busy working in the house to take time out! But the event must have been a real talking-point in the city, because all the poorer working classes, who would not have been able to afford newspapers, knew about it. It was described as 'the absorbing topic of millions in these islands'.

Another exciting event, which many remember vividly, was the fire at Leetham's flour mill in 1933. Owen Calpin saw it,

We sensed there was something very serious. We decided to clamber up the bar walls near the bar and looked towards Navigation. I don't know how long the fire had been raging but it had got a very good hold, tremendous sheets of flame roaring through the roof, proceeded by belching clouds of grey murky smoke. The heat in the vicinity must have been terrific, we even felt the blast of heat from that distance.

Pat Daker, of Ellerkers, remembers playing with,

Mary and Hetty Bean We were real good pals. Their dad used to keep pigs and guess who used to go and put her hands in wi't'taties and t'meal. Hetty and I

used to make pig meal up and then chop sticks and make them into bundles. And Mrs Bean made all her own bread and would shout over t'wall, 'Are you there Pat?' and a great big hot teacake used to come across. We would chase each other round t'Bar Walls, get off at one point and jump onto t'next. Or we used to go round shoe shops and collect shoe boxes to make little puppet shows. Take empty bottles back for t'pennies and go to the Electric. I've seen Old Mother Riley that many times, I used to go every day of the week. I can remember the old King coming down Walmgate, he came with Queen Mary in the 1940s. And I was stood in t'shop door with a cat in me hand, with a bow on its neck. I remember that vividly, I just felt a fool with this cat.

Rubye Readhead's father kept birds,

I remember my father changed the breed from Yorkshire canaries, which were beautiful, pale yellow with long tail, very elegant, sleek canary. But they weren't the best of singers so he went over to rollers. They were little, fat, bright yellow birds and they were supposed to be good singers. The best one he brought in the house and he had it in the window, he was always whistling at it and training it to sing.

I'd help to feed the birds. And the baby birds he'd feed on hard-boiled egg and arrowroot biscuits which he mashed together, he had a pestle and mortar. And I was allowed to do that. You mix them into fine powder and then put them in the little pots. And I used to love to clean out the bowl, it's quite nice is hard-boiled egg and arrowroot biscuit, quite tasty.

Maureen Aspinall remembers,

Across the road used to be the Regal pictures. I remember it was halfway through 'Bambi' and I was glued to it and crying, and t'siren went. Well me mother had to drag me out, she actually dragged me by the 'air to get me out of the pictures because I wanted to see it. It was the last night and I was playing hell when I got outside. Me mother dragged me back to Walmgate, I showed her up. At the Electric, I used to wait for a man and woman coming and say, 'Are you going into t'pictures, will you take me in?' and I used to give 'em me penny, 'cos I wasn't allowed in, I was under age. And the first time me mother took me, I went to see Betty Grable and John Payne and Don Ameche. I didn't realise it was a

picture on the screen, I thought they were behind the screen and they were gonna come out of the door and I was gonna see these lovely people.

We had no toys. Couldn't afford toys. All I wanted was a pair of roller skates and me mother could never afford to buy me them and a couple with a young lass moved into this shop and I thought I'll make friends with her, 'cos I knew she had a pair of roller skates. And she used to lend me one roller skate and I'd roll up and down Walmgate on a night. Just by meself if others had gone in, I used to reckon I was Sonja Henie.

There was no luxuries. We used to buy a lot of lozenges, Victory V's. That's why I never eat 'em now, 'cos I ate that many in t'war, I don't want to see them again. hen it was Christmas, I used to get me dad's sock with a silver threepenny bit and a book and pencils to write with. After the war, we'd never seen chocolate, we went up town and there was this Red Cross shop. We saw in t'window Easter Eggs. I always remember our Easters. We used to have little white socks on and a dress, used to meet in Walmgate and our mothers would boil us an egg. I don't know where they gorrem from in t'war, coloured, paint a face on 'em and we'd go on Castle Hill and roll 'em. Then this Easter me mother says, 'I'm gonna get you a chocolate egg'. It was just a round egg with all these lovely flowers on. It took me six months to eat it, I'd sit and look at it. I can still see that Easter egg.

Tom Rhodes,

Lived in School Street off Navigation Road. We were all funny kids, we'd do mischievous things. Hope Street would fight with Navigation Road and they used to take people's props and ashbin lids. Then, 'Have you seen the prop?' 'No mam'. 'Well what was all that noise last night?' and the props had all gone, and someone'd come and shout, 'Annie your prop's down here'.

Those days on a Sunday especially, there was a lot of pitch and toss. You'd two pennies, you tossed 'em up and bet. It's illegal 'cos you make the Queen's head ache, tossing her. You can be summonsed for that.

Tom Rhodes outside St George's Church 1996

Lillian Prior remembers,

You made your own entertainment. My father would sit, there was only the two of us, my sister on his knee and me on a cushion between his legs. And he'd sing to us.

There was one he used to sing about a little girl whose mother had died. It went, 'Into the lone graveyard she stole, over her mother's grave she knelt and prayed, take me to your arms again,' and apparently the worshippers passed by like the Good Samaritan without taking any notice of her. The song ended with her dying on her mother's grave. We used to be with tears rolling down our cheeks and we'd say, 'Oh sing that daddy, sing that daddy'.

Despite the grim situation in Walmgate, most people learned to accept and make the best of their circumstances. Dick Calpin, who lived in Rosemary Yard, met his future wife in Walmgate,

She was christened Veronica but always called Ronnie by family and friends. We were eleven years old and met at a birthday party, playing Postman's Knock.

Ronnie was always dressed nice, little crepe de chine blouses, button boots and ringlets in her hair. Someone once described her as the bonniest little lass in Walmgate, and for me, she was. When we got married, we couldn't afford a honeymoon. We went to the picture house in Fossgate and sat on the back row, that was our honeymoon!

Rosemary Place early 1900s

During the war, Ronnie worked for Handley Page, helping to clean and repair Halifax bombers, when they came back from raids, often covered in blood from the crew's injuries. A friend nicknamed Ronnie, 'Lady Halifax' for her war efforts. In the 1930s like the greater part of the population of Walmgate, the Calpin family were rehoused.

154

When Ronnie died in 1995, Dick, and their daughters Brenda and Barbara, brought her back home to Walmgate, scattering her ashes in the garden of St Denys's church.

What emerges from listening to the stories of those people who have lived in Walmgate is the fact that a whole way of life has gone. The Irish community has long since intermarried and dispersed, and the same is true of other nationalities who once had a strong identity in the city. Walmgate has also lost its identity. One man described it as 'absolutely dead' in comparison to its former self. Others tell of how they are proud to be associated with the street, despite its rough image. The sense of community is always emphasised, another feature which is largely, but not completely, lost in modern-day insular living. The 20th century phenomenon of the nuclear family, which confines us all into much smaller groups, has meant the end of a certain way of life.

Dick Calpin believes that Walmgate was a place where life was tough but worthwhile,

There was much poverty, much need and a very poor quality of life for many families. It must be a tribute to the human spirit that we survived and went on to better times, through hard work and carrying on the traditions of love and caring, for the family and the community. I know a lot of families today who are truly glad and proud to have been part of life in Walmgate. Walmgate forged our characters, our friendships, and gave us many happy memories.

About the author ...

Van Wilson is a graduate in English and American Studies, and wrote her thesis on the subject of 'Madness in 20th Century Women's Literature'. She has been involved with oral and local history for several years, and has had articles published in several magazines.

Before starting to write books, she spent eight years in bookselling and gained the Diploma in Bookselling with distinction in five subjects.

She is the author of 'The History of A Community : Fulford Road District' (1984), 'Alexina : A Woman in Wartime York' (1995) and 'Rich in all but Money : Life in Hungate 1900-1938' (1996).

Van works as administrator for a young people's theatre company, and is married with two children.

About the photographer ...

Simon I Hill gained Diplomas in Photography and Art & Design from Blackpool College of Art in 1985, and an MA in Film and Television from the London Institute in 1992. He was elected a Fellow of the Royal Society of Arts in 1989, and of the Royal Photographic Society in 1991.

He has had photographs published in many national and international journals and periodicals including *The Sunday Times Magazine*, *National Geographic Magazine*, *The Illustrated London News* and *Der Spiegel*.

As a photographer and chartered designer, Simon is Proprietor and Creative Director of Scirebröc - a design group which he founded in 1983. Simon is married with two children.

About the ARC ...

The ARC - Archaeological Resource Centre - is an award-winning hands-on exploration of archaeology for visitors of all ages, designed by the York Archaeological Trust to complement its Jorvik Viking Centre in Coppergate. Located in the beautifully restored medieval church of St Saviour, close to the Shambles, the ARC has an ever-changing programme of special exhibitions, children's activity mornings, lectures, videos and other events throughout the year.

For further information, telephone 01 904 654 324.

The ARC is open all year, including weekends and evenings for pre-booked parties of more than 10 persons. To make a party booking for the ARC or the Jorvik Viking Centre, telephone 01 904 613 711.

Open to the public: Monday to Friday   10am to 5pm
                         Saturday and Sunday   1pm to 5pm

Closed Good Friday and 18-31 December.
Last admission 4.30pm
Special opening arrangements can be made for pre-booked groups.

The ARC is a project of the York Archaeological Trust.
The Trust is a registered charity. Number 509060.